I0522160

Converting Conspiracy Theorists

Rescue Anyone From Dangerous &
Destructive Conspiracy Theories

Antonio Perez

www.escapingtherabbithole.com

DAILY GROWTH

P R E S S

www.dailygrowthpress.com

Converting Conspiracy Theorists:

Rescue Anyone From Dangerous & Destructive Conspiracy Theories

Antonio Perez

First Printing: May 1st, 2023

This book is not intended to be a replacement or substitute for therapeutic advice from a licensed mental health professional. If you feel your loved one has a serious psychiatric issue, please contact a licensed professional.

I would like to thank my editor, proof reader and formatters (Ita De Groot, Parker Hansen, and Auheduzzaman respectively.) If there are any errors currently in the book this falls squarely on me. Please let me know if you come across any errors so I can fix them for the next edition.

This book is dedicated to:

My girlfriend for putting up with me for all of these years. I love you.

My family for always being there for me, even during my darkest times.

All of my friends in the hypnosis community that have helped me to grow over the years.

And lastly, my best friend Uncle Tom. Thanks for showing me what it's like to love and be loved. I will always cherish all the fun we've had together.

Thanks for being my Hanai father and always telling me "You're my best friend too," when I tell you that you're my best friend.

About Antonio Perez

Antonio Perez is a former conspiracy theorist turned certified hypnotist and life coach. He helps friends and family members of conspiracy theorists overcome stress, anxiety, and any other issues they're experiencing as a result of their loved one.

If you're experiencing any stress, anxiety, or any other issues because your loved one is trapped in conspiracy theories, schedule your no-cost 20-minute strategy call to discover how he can help you:

www.escapingtherabbithole.com/call

Your free bonus for buying this book:

Download a guided meditation to overcome any stress or anxiety you're experiencing from your loved one that is trapped in conspiracy theories with the link below:

www.escapingtherabbithole.com/bonus

A word of warning from the author

Suppose your loved one has severe psychiatric issues or personality disorders. If this is case, the techniques in this book might not be enough.

Sure, some of the techniques are therapeutic in nature. But you'll want to seek out Doctors and therapists that are qualified to help your loved one.

My general rule of thumb is I don't want to harm anyone any further. So if they have severe issues look into getting professional help.

You can share this book with a professional therapist. Ask them if it's okay for them to try some of the strategies in this book in conjunction with their treatment plan.

Why you should read this book

There are several reasons you should read this book.

First of all, let's face it: Conspiracy theories are on the rise across the globe. They can be very dangerous, especially if they push people to engage in extreme and violent behavior.

Imagine being able to talk your loved one down from the ledge and prevent a domestic terrorist event from happening.

Secondly, conspiracy theories cause people to detach from family and friends, leading to a sense of alienation from society.

Ever watch someone becoming increasingly detached from society? While at the same time becoming even more paranoid?

On top of all of this, conspiracy theorists can be difficult to talk to. You'll need to adjust how you approach your loved one. This book will reveal how to approach your loved one and challenge their beliefs in a compassionate and respectful way.

In summary, you'll get a first-hand look at how to help your loved one escape from dangerous and destructive conspiracy theories.

Endorsements

Awesome. Antonio delivers the best of NLP, with a laser-sharp clarity, and a fun no-bullshit approach that will make sense both as a self-help guide for recovering conspiracy theorists, and as a skilled intervention handbook for those who care about conspiracy theorists.

I loved the focus on rapport and active listening before launching into all the gentle questions and reframes for helping open up another person's model of the world. There's some stuff in here that is rare in NLP circles.

And Antonio has the background to say all this – he has been deep down the rabbit hole in his past and he has the photos to prove it! If you're freaking out about a family member, if you're not sure about your own beliefs, and even if you just want to deepen your NLP skills in working with people who are a bit paranoid, this is a must read!

Perez is a skilled writer and the book really gripped me as well. The kind of stuff the world needs urgently because, as he says, conspiracy theories are no joke. Our future is at stake.

Antonio has a way of making powerful change techniques sound easy to understand. This is a book immediately useful for those who need it most.

Richard Bolstad, author of "Cognitive Clarity: Using NLP to Help People Live Sanely".

Foreword by Dr. Richard Nongard

When I first met Antonio online in 2008, he was entrenched in the world of conspiracy theories. I remember thinking to myself *"This guy is never going to snap back into reality."* Little did I know that five years later we were going to meet at Hypnothoughts Live, and everything would change.

When we finally met face-to-face for the first time, it was like a different person had taken his place—gone was the wild conspiracy theorist, replaced by a much calmer and more grounded version of himself. When I asked him what had changed since our last conversation on the hypnosis forum, he told me he had finally quit believing in conspiracy theories. Intrigued by this transformation from skeptic to critic, I encouraged him to write about it—and so began Antonio's journey as an author of this book about helping your loved ones overcoming conspiracy theories and pseudoscience beliefs.

Now here we are fifteen years later in 2023 and thanks to Antonio's writing I now have a better understanding than ever before of how someone can get sucked down into that rabbit hole in the first place. From personal experience both on my own forums and hearing Antonio's story firsthand, I'm happy to recommend this both with others what they need to be aware of if they want avoid falling prey themselves or help their friends who may already be caught up in such dangerous ideas.

Dr. Richard Nongard
Author of *The Seven Most Effective Methods of Self-Hypnosis*
TwelveWeekBook.com

Table of Contents

Introduction

Wouldn't it be great if you could snap your fingers and pull someone away from dangerous conspiracy theories?

Sadly, it's not that easy. I really wish it was. While I can't show you how to rescue your loved with a Thanos-style finger snap, I can give you some pretty powerful techniques to get the ball rolling.

With that being said, I want to thank you for buying and reading this book! This book has been a long time in the making. I've wanted to write a book for close to thirty years, but I never knew what to write about. Eventually, I landed on the perfect topic in the form of my paranoia fueled by insane conspiracy theories and unchecked mental health issues.

Can I be totally honest with you?

My English teachers would collapse from heart attacks if they read this book. A little note about my writing style and grammar.

Or lack of grammar, for that matter. I love grammar. But I don't always follow "formal grammar" rules. I start sentences with *and* & *but* for example. Commas might be out of place here and there.

Truth be told? For years I was scared of writing because of what I considered learning disabilities. Which I can safely assume is dyslexia on top of not knowing "formal grammar".

My writing style is conversational in nature; I want you to feel like you're coming along for the ride.

In this book, you'll find several techniques to rescue your loved one from conspiracy theories and cults. While these techniques are powerful, your loved one must want to change.

With that being said, you can tip the scales in your favor because the easiest way to get your loved one to change is to change yourself.

Think of it this way—every relationship you have isn't static. Relationships are a kind of system. When one part of the system gets adjusted, the rest is affected.

You know your relationship better than anyone else.

You're probably aware of the specific triggers that cause you to get angry or frustrated with your loved one.

How would you like to be in control of your emotions, thoughts, and behaviors no matter how much your loved one tries pushing your buttons?

Imagine this – you're remaining calm and peaceful when your loved one is trying to push your buttons. And before you know it? Your loved one follows suit and calms down.

Can this really be possible? You're damn right it's possible!

Despite what you might be thinking, it's possible to accomplish this. Changing how you react to your loved one will change how they respond to you.

If you have some behaviors that could be adjusted, only you'll know what they are. These behaviors might be as simple as changing how you talk to your loved one.

On the other hand, you might want to change some complex behaviors.

Keep in mind you might have to take drastic measures when changing/adjusting some of your behaviors.

If your loved one is an abusive narcissist, you might want to go no contact with them. At least for a while until they come to their senses. If you're in a co-dependent relationship with your loved one, you should work on improving that.

Good news: This is where I step up to the plate.

Hi, my name is Antonio Perez. I'm a former conspiracy theorist plagued with mental health issues turned hypnotherapist.

I managed to transform my life and my mental health issues with hypnosis and other modalities.

I used hypnosis to overcome severe trauma, let go of anxiety/panic attacks, let go of paranoid delusions, lose weight, manage my anger, reduce stress, improve my relationships, etc.

To discover how I can help you improve your relationship with your conspiracy addicted loved one, click the link below to schedule your 20-minute no-cost strategy call.

www.escapingtherabbithole.com/call

I look forward to connecting with you.

Aloha,

Antonio

P.S. Feel free to join the Conspiracy Converter Facebook group. We've got a growing group of people who are passionate about rescuing people from conspiracy theories and cults.

www.escapingtherabbithole.com/group

P.P.S. Who else wants to discover how my run-in with military on the streets of Detroit rescued me from the grips of Alex Jones? It's revealed in the next chapter.

P.P.P.S. My sense of humor is pretty dark. Keep that in mind when reading this book.

Chapter 1
Martial Law Hits the Streets of Detroit

"*So this is how it ends, and the New World Order takes over??!?*" I think to myself.

I'm ready to dart past rows of fully armed paramilitary soldiers. We're talking armed to the teeth!

Moments earlier, I was taking a regular bus ride back from computer school.

Picture this. It's 2005, and I'm on the edge of Downtown Detroit. The bus I've taken home from computer school every weekday for over a year just takes a sharp detour.

You know what it's like when you're used to a particular pattern, then suddenly it gets switched up on you?

You notice the change in a pattern immediately after it's broken.

What the hell's going on? The bus has never gone this way??!!?

I can hear this roaring sound looming over the bus. It sounds like someone is whacking and chopping at weeds with a machete.

chakk-chackk-chak-chak, chakk-chackk-chak-chak

Imagine this: it sounds almost like an automatic sprinkler, but on steroids.

Before I know it, this sound is all I can hear. It drowns out the noise of the city and engulfs the hum of the bus.

I can feel the bus starting to shake and rumble.

"What the fuck is happening?" a stranger next to me shouts as he leaps out of his seat.

I press my face against the window and see the sound's source.

Two mysterious, unmarked black helicopters hover above us. They look straight out of some covert military operations.

We're forced to stop. A barricade of fully armed guards creeps towards us. In a matter of seconds, I'm going to be face to face with these New World Order crisis actors. These paramilitary soldiers don't look anything like the U.S. military. We're talking much more deadly and sinister looking.

That's when it hits me.

"Alex Jones is right," I scream in my head. *"... They're trying to usher in martial law!"*

At this point, I know I have to rush home to warn my friends in the Truther/Patriot movement. I need to jump on Myspace to warn everyone.

I leap off the bus and start scrambling down the sidewalk right toward these fully armed guards. Somehow their sights aren't on me. They're marching down the street past the bus. Waves of panic and terror set in.

Where the fuck are they going?

Off in the distance behind these guards, I see this terrifying guy. He's straight out of a child's nightmare.

As I get closer, my chest tightens up because I know this guy. I don't know where from, but I'm scrambling through my memories to pinpoint where I know him.

"I've seen this guy before. I know I've seen him." These paranoid thoughts are circling around in my head.

He locks his eyes on me; it's clear that he's ready to square up should push come to shove. I'm about to expose this false-flag terror plot and become a hero. And this guy? He's the only thing standing in my way.

If you were to see him, you'd run for the hills. He's straight out of a horror movie. He's not a good looking guy by any stretch of the imagination.

Picture this: he looks like a hairless scrotum stretched over a skeleton with eyes bulging out of their sockets.

Not that I ever bought into the Reptilian Agenda conspiracy. But his pale skin that barely clings to his face makes him a poster boy for Lizard People Running the Planet, Inc.

As I get closer to him, my mind spins even more out of control. All sorts of paranoid thoughts are flying around in my mind.

Where do I know this guy from?

Does he see me?

What kind of sick false-flag terror operation is this?

I've seen this guy before...has he been following me around?

Is he one of the people that has been gang-stalking me because I'm exposing people to the New World Order?

My only concern is getting home to warn my fellow patriots. I'm shuffling past him as calmly as I can while every fiber of my being screams, *"Run for your life!"* My heart is crashing against my rib cage.

I don't want to catch his attention and blow my only chance to expose this terror plot.

As I'm walking past him, I catch a glimpse of his face...

Why the fuck is the actor Steve Buscemi here? I think to myself, all puzzled.

"QUIET ON THE SET!" a voice screams from a megaphone.

You're probably cracking up right about now. I was cracking up when it happened.

At that moment, I felt like the rug got pulled from underneath me.

I realized, *"EVEN HOLLYWOOD IS IN ON IT!!!"*

HA HA HA.

Just kidding.

I had walked straight onto the set for *The Island* (starring Ewan McGregor, Scarlett Johansson, and Steve Buscemi.) I didn't even realize I was on a movie set.

What kind of mental gymnastics did I have to jump through to convince myself this was a terror plot unfolding? Confirmation bias.

Confirmation bias is the tendency for our brains to see new evidence as confirmation of our existing beliefs or theories.

In other words, my brain decided what it wanted to see.

Every time I tell this story, I change it a little bit here and there. Almost to the point that I can't remember what parts really happened and what I added for dramatic effect.

Quick question for you. Have you ever told a story so many times you change bits and pieces here and there? Before you know it you can't tell what's real and what's a figment of your imagination? It's almost like a dream that you swore really happened to you. Only to find out later that it never happened.

Steve Buscemi played a vital role in this movie, but truth be told? He wasn't in this scene. At least not to my knowledge.

But it was too good not to include him. This also highlights something interesting about stories. (Especially the stories we constantly tell ourselves).

While Steve Buscemi wasn't in this scene, this event happened to me.

There have been times I've had to look back in my memory to see if he was actually there.

Now when I tell this story, I can see him in the story. The reason? I've told this story many times, with him being a crucial part of it. My brain has caused him to appear in my mind's eye.

He's become a key figure in this story I've told countless times over the past few years.

This goes for all of the stories that conspiracy theorists tell themselves and others. They start to believe these stories, despite them not being true.

Here's a fun fact about Steve Buscemi:

He worked as a firefighter for four years, starting in 1980. When the Twin Towers were attacked on September 11th, 2001, he volunteered to find survivors. He worked twelve-hour days for a week straight.

What if I had heard this about him when I was knee-deep in conspiracy theories? I can say without a shadow of a doubt a new story would have crept into my mind:

"Steve Buschemi is in on it! He's part of the false flag operation to make this look like a legit attack on American soil."

Truth be told, he's a hero for returning to the line of duty.

My confirmation bias at the time would have painted him as part of some big government plot that infiltrated Hollywood. You better believe I would have used all evidence at my disposal to prove it.

I'm glad I got slapped in the face with a dose of reality that day. This was one of the defining moments that made me realize Alex Jones was full of shit. Not to mention the whole Truther/Patriot movement.

This moment helped me start unpacking the B.S. stories I was telling myself.

Which brings up an interesting point:

Conspiracy theories paint conspiracy theorists as the victim. The enemy? The outside forces that cause the world's problems.

During my time as a paranoid conspiracy theorist, the stories I told myself had one thing in common:

I was the victim in the story. As well as the hero that could expose the New World Order.

The fear mongers who peddle conspiracy theories want their followers focused on some evil outside forces.

They want people who fall into the "It's us versus them" mindset. They frame some nefarious outside force as the cause of all of the world's problems.

This nefarious outside force is painted out to be the enemy. Conspiracy theorists are led to believe these external forces are the ones silently pulling the strings on every bad thing happening in the world.

Conspiracy theorists blame every terrible thing happening in the world on the Illuminati, New World Order, the deep state, satanic pedophiles, Jews, etc.

Ever wonder conspiracy theories are so addicting?

I've got some theories about conspiracy theories (oooh, see what I did there? It's so very meta. I could have practically written the movie Inception!)

Conspiracy theories are more prominent in people with an external rather than an internal locus of control.

Locus of control refers to an individual's perception of the leading causes of events in his or her life.

Or, more simply:

Do you believe that your destiny is controlled by yourself or external forces such as fate, God, or powerful others?

As humans, we have a lot of choices in how we show up in the world. We can either actively shape what happens in our lives. Or we can allow the outside world to shape our circumstances.

Having an external locus of control means you simply exist in the world. You're not taking deliberate actions. You just let life dictate what happens. You also tend to place blame on the outside world and outside forces:

The world sucks... I'm just an unlucky person... I was dealt a shitty hand in life.

Whereas someone with an internal locus of control takes responsibility for what happens in their life:

Okay, that goal turned out differently than I wanted. What can I do better next time to achieve my goal?

Conspiracy theories cause people to look out for danger in the outside world—a threat that might not even exist in the first place.

Take a depressed person, for example. Good chance they're being affected by life and external circumstances versus being the cause of what's happening in their life.

(**NOTE:** this is not to suggest that people with mental health issues or mental illness are acting as victims. Trauma and other horrible things can and do happen to people.)

When someone takes the initiative to do some healing work, they can switch from being affected by life to being the cause of what happens from this point forward.

According to the Journal of Mental Health and human behavior:

"Those with an external locus of control are indicative of unstable emotional patterns and behaviors, while those with an internal locus of control are more emotionally stable."

On top of this, conspiracy theories are also addicting because of the human mind's ability to connect the dots between unrelated events.

When someone's mind has an external locus of control and connects the dots between unrelated things, it's fertile ground for conspiracy theories to spring up.

But I'm jumping ahead of myself. We'll cover more about locus of control and the "connecting the dots" phenomenon in Chapter 4. You'll also discover exactly how I got sucked into conspiracy theories.

In this book, I will show you how implementing a few communication and therapeutic techniques can help rescue your loved one from conspiracy theories...by assisting them in switching from an external to an internal locus of control.

So who am I?

My name is Antonio Perez and I'm a former conspiracy theorist. For seven years, I got sucked deep into conspiracy theories and the "patriot movement."

Hell, the Michigan Militia even tried to recruit me at one point. Picture this: my cell phone starts ringing off the hook.

Ring Ring Ring

"Hello?"

"Hi, this is John from the Michigan Militia. Is this Antonio Perez?"

"Yes, it is. What's up?"

"I'd like to talk to you about joining the Michigan Militia!"

"Okay, but I'm Mexican. Will that be a problem?"

CLICK!

That phone call is pretty odd, considering John was living in Southwest Detroit at the time. Southwest Detroit is known as Mexicantown because of all the Mexican immigrants that settled there. (If you're ever in Mexicantown, go to Los Altos. Their tacos are the best around!)

My descent into madness started by getting introduced to Alex Jones (which we'll dive into in Chapter 4).

Luckily, I stumbled back onto my lifelong interest in hypnotherapy. Using hypnosis and some other modalities, I broke free from the grip of conspiracy theories.

As someone who broke free from conspiracy theories, I have a wealth of strategies and insights to share with you.

Hopefully this can open a door for your loved one to walk through and leave behind the dangerous world of conspiracy theories/cults.

As a hypnotherapist and life coach, I help people break free from the anxiety that can make them prone to believing in conspiracy theories in the first place.

I personally hate the term "life coach." It sounds super cringey if you ask me. And even if you didn't ask me, you're still gonna get that answer ¯_(ツ)_/¯

Before we move on let's do a quick recap:

The big idea behind this book is an external locus of control, and connecting the dots between unrelated events is the most significant reason people get sucked into conspiracy theories.

Believe it or not, when someone shifts from an external to an internal locus of control, they can loosen the grip of conspiracy theories.

"Is this really possible?"

You bet it is!

In fact, in the next chapter, I will cover the F.A.M.E. Addiction mindset that has kept your loved one stuck in conspiracy theories.

You ready to get the ball rolling? See you in the next chapter!

Chapter 2
The F.A.M.E. Addiction to conspiracy theories

We've made history! I'm standing here in awe, looking over the crowd of people cheering us on.

As a movement, we are showing the New World Order that we are a force that cannot be fucked with.

You can hear cheering as we chase the oppressors and tyrants down the halls.

Glass shattering all around us symbolizes the tearing down of these tyrants.

"These are the bloodsucking deep-state enemies Alex Jones warned us about for years!" I scream in my head.

In fact, Alex was with us to fight; with his bullhorn in hand, he rallied the troops.

"We have only begun to resist the globalists. We have only begun to fight against their tyranny. They have tried to steal this election in front of everyone!" Alex screams from his bullhorn.

The crowd grows restless—pent-up rage ready to explode.

"I don't know how this is all going to end, but if they want a fight, they better believe they've got one!"

The Hillbilly Hunger Games is in full effect on January 6th. There are glass and broken bits of the Capitol in the wake of us taking power back from the Globalists. All hell has broken loose.

Wanna know a secret?

I wasn't at the Capitol on January 6th 2021. I watched the terror unfold on TV from the comfort of my home because we were in a global pandemic. And I'm not some weirdo that will mold my identity to match that of a president.

In other words, I'm not a member of a cult.

The reason for telling the fictional story?

To illustrate the grip conspiracy theories have on people. More so, the power they hold over groups of people that mobilize.

Conspiracy theories wield immense power over people. Especially when these people begin to meet up in real life.

This starts to validate their ideas.

"See, I'm not crazy after all! Other people believe this stuff!"

Meeting up in person also feeds into the idea that they've somehow *tapped into some secret information.*" After all, as I mentioned above, other people believe it. So it makes it more realistic in their minds.

Once conspiracy theorist's meet each other in person, they feel like they're part of something much bigger.

Why do you think Trump's rallies were so popular? And full of a shit ton of QAnon members?

QAnon cult members are constantly talking about "the great awakening." They feel like they're part of some great movement that will shine a light on these nefarious forces running the world.

It gives them purpose and meaning. Make no bones about it, it only gets worse from here.

Had I not left Alex Jones' cult in 2008, I would have ended up at the Capitol.

I could have easily been radicalized like the over 2,000 people that descended on the Capitol.

Trump's "big lie" took root in the minds of millions of people. What would have been the outcome if those people weren't told that big lie in the first place?

Have you ever wonder what would've happened if those people operated from an internal locus of control? As opposed to seeing the world as a dangerous place that's out to get them?

A place they thought wanted to take away their freedom.

Could January 6th have turned out differently if those people weren't primed to see conspiracy theories around every corner?

Could the techniques and concepts we're about to dig into have helped pull them out of conspiracy theories?

Now that January 6th has happened, we know it can happen again. All bets are off. Especially with politicians that are spreading conspiracy theories.

Please make me a promise.

Read this book all the way through. Discover the tools you can use to rescue your loved one from conspiracy theories.

The longer someone is exposed to conspiracy theories, the greater their chance of becoming indoctrinated.

Hundreds of people were led to the slaughter on January 6th by a president who hawked conspiracy theories left and right.

Together we can work to help people escape dangerous conspiracy theories, not to mention stamp out misinformation. Just know that switching from an external to an internal locus of control isn't enough.

Here's your secret weapon to fight back against conspiracy theories:

The F.A.M.E. Addiction Model

There are a few factors that keep people from escaping conspiracy theories:

1) Feeling powerless and wanting to be seen as a hero

Conspiracy theorists often feel powerless and insignificant. Many conspiracy theorists are looking for something missing in their lives; be it happiness, significance, respect, etc.

Having some sort of secret "insider knowledge" is very alluring.

A conspiracy theory can take a person from feeling insignificant to feeling like they have come from the mountaintop with information that can save the world.

Ultimately they want to be seen as a hero in a battle between good and evil.

Luckily you'll discover some simple techniques to help your loved one feel more significant.

2) Apophenia

"App o fee what nee uh?"

Ahem. For us common folk, it means connecting the dots.

It's a fancy-sounding word that means "to perceive a connection or meaningful pattern between unrelated or random things."

One of the biggest reasons people get stuck digging into conspiracies is apophenia. Basically, it's connecting the dots between things. We've briefly touched on this so far.

A common trait conspiracy theorists share is connecting the dots between random events. Before you know it, a complex story is formed in their mind.

It's always a complex story. The reason is simple. When a big event happens, we like to think it requires an equally big complex cause. So conspiracy theorists will connect-the-dots and create a wild fantasy.

This story can often get stuck in a conspiracy theorist's head, almost like an ear worm (those songs that get stuck in your head and you can't get rid of). They're looking for a grand story to explain seemingly complex events.

Sound far-fetched to you? It's not. Here's why:

Humans are "meaning-making" machines. We're constantly attaching meanings to all sorts of things.

"She smiled at me, so that means she likes me."

"My wife yelled at me. She must not love me anymore."

The thing about apophenia is that it makes our beliefs even more solid. When you connect the dots yourself, you are more likely to believe the meaning you've made than if someone told you what something meant or what to believe.

There's a reason Alex Jones tells people, *"Don't trust me, do your own research."*

He wants you to generate the beliefs in your mind. It makes the beliefs a lot sturdier.

By the way, telling a person, "Don't trust me, do your own research," makes you seem more trustworthy. This is a common sales and influence technique.

"Don't trust me about our product. Head over to our competitors to compare us."

A salesperson telling you to "shop around" is similar to Alex Jones saying, "Don't trust me, do your own research."

He becomes more trustworthy when he tells you not to trust him. It makes it easier to persuade someone to believe what you want them to believe. Let's be honest. Alex Jones is giving you the dots to connect. He's setting everything up so you can easily make the connections.

His basic formula is to feed you some loose "facts" and tell you not to trust him but to do your own research. This gets the ball rolling.

But that's just the tip of the iceberg.

Another popular strategy Alex Jones uses to sow seeds of doubt is by asking questions like this:

"If we were lied to about what happened on 9/11, what else did they lie to us about?"

This question is powerful because it presupposes a couple of things. It makes the following assumptions:

1. The person pushing the conspiracy theory is correct.

2. There are other things they could be right about.

This causes conspiracy theorists to ask themselves this very question. In addition, they start asking themselves the following question:

"If he was right about X, what else is he right about?"

This question starts to prop up Alex Jones as some sort of boy wonder. He's seen as the person that's cracked the case on the Deep State.

These questions cause them to look for evidence proving the conspiracy theory right (as well as proving Alex Jones right). They start their research with a conclusion in mind and search for evidence to back it up.

Guess what happens when you do the research and connect-the-dots like he suggested? You get a rush of dopamine and other feel-good chemicals.

In turn, you associate Alex Jones with that rush of happy chemicals. You start to see him as the person who caused that dopamine rush.

Next up we've got...

3) Misinformation

Misinformation isn't new. It's always been a thing.

What's new is the prolific nature of social media. Social media's ability to spread misinformation is unmatched even by governments that have spread propaganda far and wide. Hell, despotic governments of old would have wished for social media.

A fascist or dictatorial government and people don't need to censor information. They can simply flood a ton of information for people to digest.

Did Trump have to censor any information to get the big lie spreading? Nope, he just had to pump the big lie over and over.

We get information in bite-sized chunks. Social media companies make it devastatingly simple to spread stuff like wildfire.

It can be challenging for someone prone to conspiratorial thinking to break away from misinformation.

And it doesn't help that social media creates echo chambers. Echo chambers. Echo chambers. Echo chambers.

Sorry, I couldn't resist the bad joke :D

Social media feeds into these echo chambers. It shows us more of what we're already being exposed to.

4) External vs. internal locus of control

The concept of locus of control is psychological. We can have either an internal or external locus of control. This describes how a person may assign what or who controls their lives.

Someone with an internal locus of control believes they are responsible for what happens in their life. An external locus of control causes people to see outside forces controlling their life.

5) Addiction

Conspiracy theories are very addicting.

A common phenomenon with conspiracy theories is "doing research" to uncover new discoveries. When someone uncovers a new conspiracy, they get a mini-high. They get rewarded with dopamine, which is part of our brains reward system.

It's evolutionary biology that's extremely hard to resist.

This is why conspiracy theorists will send you on wild goose chases under the guise of *"doing your own research."* They want you to experience the same dopamine rush they got from uncovering a conspiracy.

A common misconception is they tell you to *"do your own research"* because they don't have a good source. Which is usually the case. But the reason behind them doing this is that they want you to make the connection yourself.

Because if you're spoon-fed a specific idea or belief, it doesn't hold the same weight as if you were to connect the dots on your own.

You have the added one-two combo of getting a mini-hit of dopamine and making the connection yourself.

A conspiracy theorist is rewarded with dopamine by uncovering a conspiracy or at least making the connections in their brain.

Humans are constantly trying to make meanings out of their experiences. If you're getting a hit of dopamine and you're connecting the dots between two unrelated things, it's much more powerful.

A conspiracy theorist doesn't want to deprive you of the joy of uncovering a conspiracy or making the connections they also made in their minds:

Why should I just give this information up so easily? I had to do the hard work and discover it myself. They should be required to as well. After all, I would deprive them of the satisfaction of putting all the pieces together!

Rest assured, these five factors can be overcome, as you'll soon discover.

Before we jump to how I broke free from conspiracy theories and how you can help others do the same, we need to talk about something terrifying.

If you don't read on to discover how to help someone break free from conspiracy theories, your loved one will remain stuck. They'll fall deeper into the conspiracy rabbit hole. Imagine how much worse they'll be when their anxiety and depression go unchecked.

Best case scenario? They'll remain glued to the internet, going on wild goose chases.

Worst case? They may find themselves trying to play "hero army guy" in the real world.

One of Alex Jones' followers went to a pizza joint in Washington, D.C. He was enraged that politicians were molesting kids and killing them in satanic rituals.

He was armed with an AR-15 to kill satanic pedophiles molesting kids; not to mention harvesting adrenochrome from their blood. Which obviously wasn't happening. Thank God he was caught before he hurt anyone.

That's the absolute worst case. But do you really want to wait around until it gets that bad?

Now is the time to pull your loved one back from the abyss. Don't let your loved ones fall prey to these merchants of fear. Read on to discover how to rescue them from dangerous and destructive conspiracy theories.

Just reading this book isn't enough. You need to use this book's practical tools and exercises.

To recap, the five obstacles to escaping conspiracy theories are:

- Feeling powerless and wanting to be seen as a hero
- Apophenia (connecting the dots)
- Misinformation
- External vs. internal locus of control
- Addiction to conspiracy theories

F.A.M.E. Addiction is a fitting acronym when you think about it. Conspiracy theorists are looking for fame and recognition. They want to be seen as heroes. At the same time, they are literally addicted to uncovering new "information."

Has someone you cared for struggled with any of these obstacles?

Watching someone you care about butting up against these obstacles can be difficult.

You can see these obstacles clear as day. They shut down no matter how much you try to steer them the right way. If only you could open their eyes to the manipulation they've endured. You'll have to take a unique approach to communicate with someone drowning in conspiracy theories.

From my experience as a hypnotist, I can recommend some great ways to create this opening by creating an open dialogue. We'll cover this soon.

For now, realize that you're not alone. There are a ton of people who have been manipulated. That's the bad news.

Fear is a powerful motivator. Alex Jones, Rush Limbaugh, Fox News, Tucker Carlson, Newsmax, O.A.N., all know this. They all peddle fear porn to the tune of millions of dollars. Alex Jones' financial's showed he raked in over $800,000 daily at one point.

Honestly, it's more ethical to sell heroin than to make money off the back of slain Sandy Hook children.

Enough with the doom and gloom. The good news is you can pull your loved ones back from conspiracies and the monsters that push them.

Imagine discovering a handful of concepts and techniques to nip this problem in the bud. Imagine bringing your loved ones back from the pit of despair...to a place where they're mentally and emotionally grounded, not dominated by anxious or paranoid thoughts.

You're about to sink your teeth into techniques and strategies to rescue your loved one from the dark world of conspiracy theories.

Do your loved one a huge favor. Have an open mind. You may come across some concepts that seem bizarre. Or an idea that is difficult to wrap your mind around. Just bear with me. I promise the pieces will all fall together.

Here are some frequently asked questions:

- Can I influence someone to change if I don't know hypnosis?

Absolutely! In fact, you might be in a better position. You see, hypnotists love getting wrapped up in the techniques we use. Sometimes we can overthink and complicate things.

With just a few simple adjustments to your communication, you'll be on the right path in no time!

- What if someone doesn't want to change? Can I still help them to change?

I'm not going to lie. If someone doesn't want to change, it'll be more difficult. But don't despair. You'll discover a few ways to overcome someone's reluctance to change.

Just bust out the Instant Influence pattern in Chapter 14 to get the ball rolling. Or gently shift their beliefs with some questions from Chapter 10.

- What if someone is dead set on arguing with me about some conspiracy theory or shoving it down my throat?

Not a problem. The techniques in Chapter 8 can help you remain calm and emotionally neutral.

- What if we are opposed politically?

If you're willing to set aside your political differences for a few moments, you can still help your loved ones. The strategies in Chapter 8 can help with this.

- What if someone seems to have far-out crazy ideas?

The good news is you've got access to a powerful technique to help someone detox from toxic and harmful thought patterns in Chapter 13.

I want to finish this chapter on a high note. Your loved one can bounce back from conspiracy theories.

Sure, the future might seem bleak now, but just know that your loved one can escape from conspiracy theories.

You'll get up close and personal with the insane thoughts and beliefs I had at the time. After all, I was able to get out alive. And believe me, I was in over my head.

So, if you're ever frustrated and don't feel like you're making progress with your loved one, take a moment to think about how much you love them.

Do this for them. Hell, do this for society. Together we can pull people back from scumbags like Alex Jones. They peddle conspiracies to the tune of millions of dollars.

So, keep pushing through this book. Dig into my perspective as a former conspiracy theorist so you can better understand what it's like on the other side.

I'm excited to take you on this journey!

Are you ready to discover what these powerful techniques are? They're all listed in the next chapter.

Chapter 3
Overview of the Solutions in This Book

Can I be totally honest with you? I almost gave up on writing this book because I wanted to cram way too much stuff in this book.

It became very overwhelming. So I had to pick what I thought were the most powerful techniques and toss the rest.

With that being said, let's push on.

The last chapter had a bit of doom and gloom. But fear not weary traveler. You're about to discover the tools to help someone break free from the grip of conspiracy theories.

While breaking away from conspiracy theories seems almost impossible, there are solutions.

We'll touch briefly on these solutions below:

Chapter 4: How I Fell Down the Rabbit Hole

You'll learn the exact moment I got pulled into conspiracy theories. We'll take a more in depth peek at the psychology principle known as Locus of Control. This is one of the key deciding factors in determining whether or not someone is prone to conspiracy thinking.

Chapter 5: Real-World Consequences of Conspiracies

This isn't so much a how-to chapter full of techniques. Instead, it's a hard look at the effect conspiracy theories have in the real world, from tearing apart families to causing acts of violence.

Chapter 6: What's Your Motivation for Reading This Book?

While this book is primarily about helping your loved one to change, this chapter is all about you.

We'll dig into the motivations behind helping rescue your loved ones from conspiracy theories.

On top of this, I'll guide you through a simple mental exercise to achieve your goals; the goals you have about rescuing your loved one from conspiracy theories.

Chapter 7: My Conspiracy Theory Daze

Up next, we'll dive into the world of psychology. You'll discover key concepts to help you understand where your loved one might be coming from.

These concepts can also better explain their motivations for getting wrapped up in conspiracy theories.

You don't have to agree with anyone about their beliefs. But you can respect that their ideas and their model of the world do something for them.

It might make little sense now, yet once you dig into these concepts, it will make a ton of sense.

Chapter 8: Keep Calm When Talking to Your Loved One

You have to tread lightly when jumping into a conversation with a conspiracy theorist or cult member. You'll want to leave any negative judgments at the door. At the same time, you'll need to remain compassionate and curious about where your loved one is coming from.

This will be easy to do when you implement the exercises in this chapter.

Have you ever found yourself in a heated argument with someone about conspiracy theories? If so, you'll get a lot out of this chapter.

Chapter 9: Two Skills To Rescue Conspiracy Theorists

You'll need to build and maintain rapport to rescue your loved one from conspiracy theories.

This chapter has a few simple ways to build strong levels of rapport as well as rekindle rapport that might have been lost or damaged.

Chapter 10: Conspiracy Converting Questions

Questions are a pivotal part of being human. We ask ourselves questions every single day. The kinds of questions we ask ourselves influence our behaviors and our thoughts.

You'll discover powerful questions that can rapidly shift your loved one's beliefs.

Chapter 11: The Hidden Benefits Technique

Every behavior we engage in has some kind of hidden benefit. This goes for everyone—conspiracy theorists, non-conspiracy theorists, you, me, etc.

Ever engaged in a harmful habit even though you know it's bad for you?

Logically, you know it's terrible for you. But deep down, something keeps you engaged in that habit or behavior. We've all engaged in self-sabotaging behavior at one time or another. Is it because we're not smart? Not in the slightest. All behaviors do something for us, no matter how destructive it is. They serve some kind of emotional need.

Psychologists call it the "function of the behavior." As in, what kind of function does the behavior serve?

You'll learn a concept that states, "Behind every behavior, there is a positive intention." Don't confuse this with whether or not a behavior is good or bad.

A behavior can be destructive, like smoking, and still do something positive for you emotionally speaking.

You'll discover a simple way to uncover why your loved one is engaged in conspiracy theories.

This technique can help them *short-circuit* their minds allowing them to get this hidden benefit without falling down conspiracy theory rabbit holes.

Chapter 12: Conspiracy Theory Craving Buster

Remember how we talked about how conspiracy theories are addicting because they pump dopamine into our bodies?

This is our brain's reward system at play.

A conspiracy theorist's brain is wired to seek out and "uncover" new conspiracies.

As discussed in Chapter 2, when new conspiracies are "discovered," they flood dopamine into the body. You'll get your hands on a technique to help them break that addictive dopamine cycle.

This technique can break the addictive and obsessive cycle that conspiracy theorists have with social media, smartphones, and misinformation websites.

We'll also discuss a way to turn this technique into a game with your loved one. So instead of being addicted to the things that drag them further into conspiratorial thinking, they'll be hooked on winning this simple game.

Chapter 13: How to Stop Paranoid and Anxious Thoughts

One thing conspiracy theorists all have in common are thoughts filled with fear. Fear of the unknown, fear of shadow governments, and so on and so forth.

Letting go of these thoughts is key to their recovery.

You'll discover a simple exercise to help them let go of these thoughts. Five to ten minutes of daily practice can help them break free for good!

One of the benefits of this technique is that it will help detach and unravel the stories your loved ones have been telling themselves.

This is one of the best emotional regulation tools you'll find. This tool alone can help your loved ones switch from an external to an internal locus of control.

Remember that an external locus of control takes all your power away. In contrast, an internal locus of control places you directly in control of how you show up in the world.

Chapter 14: Motivate a Conspiracy Theorist to Change

It's expected that you'll experience some resistance. Resistance to change is not uncommon among conspiracy theorists. I'll be blunt: no one likes change—not your conspiracy addicted loved one, not you, and definitely not me.

So sometimes we need a little push.

This chapter has two easy-to-implement strategies to motivate someone to change.

Chapter 15: The Next Steps in Your Journey

You've just read a primer about what this book covers.

I want to state an important point:

From this point forward, it's your decision to keep reading this book.

You don't have to do anything you don't want to. You're an adult and can make your own decisions. Important decisions that can affect your loved one trapped in conspiracy theories.

At this point, you're at a fork in the road. There is one of two decisions you can make.

Decision 1: You can stop reading this book. Who knows? You might stumble onto some of these techniques on your own.

You can also invest the thousands of dollars and countless hours I dropped into hypnosis training over the years.

You can also jump headfirst into Alex Jones' cult of crazy and learn how to bring yourself out of conspiratorial thinking like I did. Talk about unnecessary on-the-job experience!

Better yet?

Decision 2: Keep reading this book. Discover how to toss a life preserver to someone drowning in a sea of conspiracy theories.

You and I both know what you need to do. Do your loved ones and society a huge favor and dive headfirst into this potentially lifesaving book.

Do you want to learn how a chance encounter in a seedy bar sent me down the Alex Jones rabbit hole? The next chapter covers this in graphic detail.

Chapter 4
How I Fell Down the Rabbit Hole

Ever wonder why some people fall for Alex Jones BS while others laugh him off?

You'll uncover a concept known as F.A.M.E. Addiction in this chapter that explains this.

But first, let's look at how I got introduced to Alex Jones:

"Have you ever heard of Alex Jones?" this rough biker-looking guy asked me. *"He's waging war on the New World Order, and bringing freedom back to America."*

As that last line dropped, he tapped the pocket Constitution poking out of his front pocket.

(Here's a hint: if someone has a pocket Constitution, take everything they say with a grain of salt. It's a HUGE red flag.)

For the next hour or so, he schooled me. Schooled me on what you ask? Alex Jones, the New World Order, the Illuminati, shadow governments, and more. I was utterly blown away by his knowledge. Imagine getting all this information at once. I was drinking straight from the fire hose.

Everything started to make sense; my perception of reality shattered, stirring me from my slumber.

For years I struggled with debilitating depression and anxiety. No kind of treatment made the slightest bit of difference. Then all of a sudden, this stranger lifted the veil.

I felt powerless and insignificant in my life. Then this stranger showed up out of nowhere and gave me a sliver of hope.

I went home that afternoon and started devouring Alex Jones' "documentaries."

Think about it like this. I saw the outside world as a messed up and depressing place.

Then all of a sudden, I discovered that shadow governments were pulling the strings behind natural disasters, mass shootings, etc.

From that point forward, I was on a mission. No, a quest. A quest to help expose the New World Order.

Growing up as a victim of bullying, I embarked on a quest to fight back. The New World Order was in my sights. They were the ultimate schoolyard bullies. All of us "common folk" were victims.

Imagine having a past where you felt powerless, weak, and insignificant. Maybe you were constantly bullied. Next toss in some trauma for good measure.

Now when you see a perceived threat from a sinister unseen force, your defenses shoot up.

You aim to protect others and earn recognition as a hero by exposing what's happening in the world.

You start making connections and attaching significance to all sorts of random events. I'm getting ahead of myself, we'll get more into the psychology behind this in a bit, but let's keep pushing on.

Over the next seven years, I got sucked into the conspiracy/patriot movement. What could have happened if I hadn't had second thoughts about conspiracy theories? I could have ended up at the Capitol on January 6th, 2021.

Imagine being dragged down a very dark path—a path that is a self-fulfilling prophecy.

You know the drill. The more you look into conspiracies, the deeper you fall down the rabbit hole.

Luckily, my lifelong interest in mind-expanding modalities (hypnosis, NLP, meditation, etc.) helped to break the spell conspiracies had on me.

When someone feels powerless or out of control, and they have an external locus of control, conspiracy theories can be very seductive.

They're seductive because they take the focus off their mental health. It causes them to see the New World Order, Illuminati, etc., as the cause of their internal struggles.

Conspiracy theorists are in a toxic relationship with conspiracy theories. They've become victims of the nefarious forces they think they're fighting against.

While conspiracy theorists think they are getting control when they uncover conspiracies, they are just reinforcing their toxic relationship with conspiracy theories.

They want to be the heroes who expose these nefarious forces.

No matter what happens, they can't seem to break free from this relationship. It's like looking at a train wreck. You don't want to stare, but you can't look away.

On top of this, anytime a new conspiracy is "exposed," they become even more addicted to conspiracy theories. And from here it keeps getting worse.

God forbid if they share some revelation on social media, and it spreads like wildfire. All of the shares, likes, and comments reinforce their beliefs.

Our brains LOVE novelty. We get flooded with dopamine when exposed to something new and fresh.

Back to what I mentioned earlier that keeps your loved one stuck in conspiracy theories:

F.A.M.E. Addiction

Feeling powerless and insignificant

Apophenia (connecting the dots)

Misinformation

External locus of control

Addiction to conspiracy theories

We're facing a dire problem. Many people have been lured into the dangerous world of conspiracy theories.

Let me guess? You've probably seen someone get sucked in, often becoming so entrenched in these illogical theories.

Luckily, there are ways to rescue them from the clutches of conspiracy theories. It definitely helps if someone is on the fence and already beginning to rethink their beliefs and ideas.

There's still hope, even for people firmly in the grips of conspiracy theories.

The biggest point I want to make is this:

People who have underlying mental health issues are more prone to falling prey. Yes, I know it's probably obvious to you. But stay with me, we're gonna cover this in a little bit.

But first:

Let's touch on the Locus of Control concept mentioned earlier:

A person can take an active role in how their life plays out. Or they can be passive and controlled by outside forces.

In other words, will someone be driving their own car, deciding where they want to go in life?

Or will they be the passenger and just sit back and take a passive role in life?

When we take an active role, we are "being at cause" for what happens. We're taking ownership of what we experience in life.

Psychologists call this **locus of control**. It's a fancy way of saying where you put your location of control. Another way to think of it is, "Where am I putting my power?"

You can either have an internal or external locus of control.

An internal locus of control is commonly called "being at cause." This is the concept that we, as opposed to external forces, have control of our life.

Focusing on conspiracy theories as the cause of suffering in the world, and your own personal suffering, is an example of an **external locus of control**.

An external locus of control is commonly referred to as "being at effect."

While focusing on conspiracy theories can make a person feel like they are in control, it reinforces an external locus of control. Conspiracy theorists tend to see outside forces as the cause of their suffering. It becomes a toxic self-fulfilling prophecy.

News flash: conspiracy theories are a depressed person's best friend.

Please put the pitchforks down! Just hear me out on this.

Conspiracy theories help people stop thinking about their problems for a little while; it's a kind of survival mechanism.

It comes down to evolutionary biology. These theories fulfill a need to feel safe and protected. As well as feeling powerful and significant.

Take someone who is experiencing depression for example. Instead of digging into what's causing their depression, conspiracy theories allow them to shift blame to the outside world. Rather than seeing their depression as originating from inside them, they can place blame on sinister forces.

And every time they "uncover" a new conspiracy, they get pulled further from the truth; their unchecked mental health issues are at the core of what's keeping them stuck.

An interesting phenomenon of conspiracy theories is apophenia. Apophenia is when someone "connects the dots" between unrelated things.

Once we start connecting the dots, our minds hit the ground running.

Take someone with mental health issues and get them to connect the dots, and you can send them falling down the rabbit hole.

Now take a moment and think about the story I opened this chapter with.

I was emotionally fragile and vulnerable. I didn't have any explanations as to why my life sucked. I just wanted to be free from depression and anxiety.

As soon as I got introduced to Alex Jones, my brain started to make connections between all sorts of unrelated things. Things that had absolutely no connection to one another. Before I knew it, I was off to the races.

This can happen to the best of us, especially when we're in a vulnerable and fragile mental state.

Next, our mind creates a story about why things happened the way they did. Or we whip up a fantasy about what will happen in the future. We've attached a meaning that might not be true.

I have something rather embarrassing to admit:

When I fell down the conspiracy theory rabbit hole, I started to believe some anti-Semitic conspiracy theories.

It didn't happen overnight.

What if I'd been introduced to the idea that "Jews are running the world" right off the bat? I would have laughed this off.

Instead, I was introduced to a more plausible conspiracy theory:

9/11 was an inside job.

Conspiracy theories are like pyramid schemes. At first, your friend invites you to a meeting about a "business opportunity."

"Just keep an open mind, okay?" your friend tells you.

Before you know it, you're fully invested in the pyramid scheme. The same goes for conspiracy theories and cults.

The sunk-cost fallacy makes it hard to escape. We don't want to think we wasted a bunch of time on something.

Well, I've already invested a lot of time and energy. I can't back out now. What would my friends think of me if I quit now?

This can explain why people stay in toxic relationships for years.

I've already invested so much time. It would be stupid to quit now.

Conspiracy theorists operate much in the same way.

Imagine you're feeling powerless and out of control. Next you meet a group of people who share your same views. You get a sense of community and shared identity.

You finally feel like you belong and have a purpose in life. Not to mention they have a common cause:

To expose satanic pedophiles, or whatever flavor of crazy it is that day.

So, they'll do anything to preserve their identity. What would happen if the rug were pulled out from underneath them? Their whole identity would be shattered.

Speaking of identity, check out this picture below. This is me at the height of worshipping Alex Jones. My identity was wrapped up in the "Truther" movement. At the time I identified as a 9/11 Truther.

My entry into the conspiracy theory "pyramid scheme" was 9/11 being an inside job.

Did I jump in believing everything Alex Jones was saying? Hell no! Well not at first. It was a gradual slope.

Jones does an excellent job at convincing people. Sure, he has to use misinformation, twist the facts, and use logical fallacies. That's neither here nor there.

Being convinced 9/11 was an inside job laid the groundwork for bigger conspiracy theories to take root in my mind. At one point, I ended up on a plain looking website. This website was critical of Jews. But hear me out for a second.

This website had clear evidence the Jews were the ones pulling the strings behind everything.

The evidence? They had access to a document called The Protocols of the Elders of Zion.

"What is this document?" you ask.

It was a Jewish plan for world domination—taking over the banks, introducing liberalism, enslaving non-Jews, etc.

Only problem?

It was a complete fabrication—a hoax that was published by the Russian government in 1905. Unfortunately, I stumbled on this document in the mid-2000s. And by this time, I was obsessed with conspiracy theories. I spent damn near every waking minute on the internet "doing my own research."

As I said, I wasn't introduced to the idea, *"The Jews are satanic and are trying to enslave the world."* My introduction to conspiracies was 9/11 being an inside job.

Soon after, I stumbled onto a video that "debunked" myths about the Holocaust.

Ok I know what you're thinking:

"You were watching a video by a Neo-Nazi white supremacist!"

Not at all. That couldn't be farther from the truth. David Cole, a Jewish filmmaker, recorded and produced this low-budget documentary. I'm using "documentary" very loosely.

Looking back, it was a shoddy attempt at film making.

Part of what made it so convincing is a Jewish person produced it. It gave more credibility than some hillbilly Klan member making it. It also allowed me to entertain the thought *I'm not racist or anti-Semitic because a Jewish person made this.*

We would never get people of color promoting racist and anti-Semitic right-wing talking points, right?

Candace Owens and Kanye enter the building.

"Here, hold our beers"

I get disgusted when I remember how I used to entertain anti-Semitic talking points.

If someone tried to call me out on my anti-Semitic bullshit, I'd think *"I can't be anti-Semitic because I like Arabs."* Because technically, Arabs are Semitic people.

I'd also try to defend my anti-Semitism by saying, *"I have never had any bad experiences with Arabs. Jews were the ones I had a problem with growing up."*

The reason for this is I went to school in Huntington Woods, Michigan. This is a primarily Jewish area of Michigan.

And guess what? I just happened to be bullied a bit when I was a kid.

I unconsciously placed blame on all Jews for being bullied. When exposed to the idea that Jews were running the world, I knew where to focus my anger.

Luckily, I rescued myself from conspiracy theories before I got in too deep.

In the first chapter we took a deep dive into how I stumbled into what I thought was a false flag terror drill. Only to discover it was a movie set. Talk about embarrassing!

Let's dig a little deeper into the next thing that pulled me out of crazy town:

It's 2007. A husband and wife out of New Hampshire were caught up in tax evasion. Ed and Elaine Brown had been fighting against the Feds for a few years.

Ed Brown was a real piece of work. Sure, now I know he was a piece of shit. But at the time? Not so much.

Alex Jones propped this guy up as a patriot fighting against the globalists. Many of Jones' followers went to Ed's compound in New Hampshire to show support.

Word on the street is an informant was lurking on Stormfront, a notorious white supremacist internet forum.

If I remember correctly, this informant brought supplies to the Brown's compound. One of these supplies was a "secure" satellite phone to help them keep connected just in case the Feds shut off their landline. Supposedly this secure satellite phone was provided by the government.

HA HA HA

They got hoodwinked by a federal informant. This might be a tall tale I heard from another conspiracy wingnut.

I know U.S. Marshals appeared as supporters and entered their house in October 2007. Once there, they discovered bombs, weapons, and booby traps.

The one thing that sticks out most about this experience was listening to Alex Jones' show in 2007. He was covering the Ed and Elaine Brown saga.

At one point, federal agents were sitting out in the woods. I believe they had positioned themselves to raid the house.

There were gunshots during the Alex Jones live broadcast from the Brown's compound. I'm not sure if it was from someone in the house or law enforcement.

This was a wake-up call for me. People could have been killed. Hell, some of my "patriot" friends got arrested for their involvement.

All because some racist knucklehead militia nut job refused to pay his income taxes. Ed Brown shouted right-wing talking points to anyone who would listen.

Since his wife was released early in 2022, she has expressed remorse for her actions. Elaine was embarrassed she let Ed control her that much. He was a loser that sponged off her.

According to Elaine Brown's children, Ed stopped working after moving in with her. This is the same person who likely bitched about immigrants taking advantage of the system.

Looking back, I was exhausted at this point in my "career" as a conspiracy theorist. I was always on high alert because Alex Jones whips his audience into a manic frenzy. He keeps people paranoid, looking out for all sorts of events that would be happening.

Eventually, I realized these things would not happen, no matter how much I wanted them to be true.

It's fifteen years later, and the New World Order still hasn't tossed my ass into a FEMA camp. (But if they manage to haul us away, I get the top bunk!)

Before we end this chapter let's rewind and look at two key points:

- The big idea in this book is an external locus of control is the most significant contributor to being prone to conspiracy theories.
- Even more importantly, when you help your loved ones shift to an internal locus of control, you can loosen the grip of conspiracy theories.

So do yourself, your loved ones, and society a favor—keep reading to discover how to push back on dangerous conspiracy theories as well as how to help your loved ones reclaim their lives.

For years I wanted to meet Alex Jones and call him out for spreading his hate-filled bullshit. Luckily, I ran into him on Kaua'i in June 2022. He went into a mini rant when I told him I quit listening to him when I stopped being paranoid.

Watch the video here by going to the link or scanning the QR code:

www.escapingtherabbithole.com/alex

Chapter 5
Real-World Consequences of Conspiracy Theories

You know what I'm sick and tired of hearing? That things like flat earth conspiracy theories are harmless fun. The fact of the matter is they open the doorway for other conspiracy theories to take root.

Conspiracy theories have real-world effects. Unfortunately, over the past few years, extremists have taken matters into their own hands. From armed attacks at pizza joints, attacks on political opponents of Trump, and even attacking the families of slain Sandy Hook children.

This chapter isn't so much filled with practical tips to rescue conspiracy theorists. Instead, you'll get a quick peek at the tragic consequences of conspiracy theories.

Before we dive in, I have a pretty crazy story to share with you.

Warning: This story is pretty damn cringeworthy. If you look at your old self and you ain't cringin', you ain't growin'.

You're about to read a call I transcribed with a fellow 9/11 Truther/Patriot from 2006.

We created the Truth Information Network. It was a way for conspiracy theorists on Myspace to network with one another. We wanted to prep for a "shit hits the fan" scenario.

It's funny how we were worried the government would track us and toss us into FEMA camps. We were actually creating a database they could use to track and follow us.

"Really think logically with that plan you guys did not." Yoda would have said.

I called my friend about a blimp flying over the Detroit Tigers stadium in February 2006. I was convinced that some shady government operation was underway during Super Bowl.

I told Drew I'd been filming this surveillance blimp flying over Tiger Stadium since 3:15 in the morning.

Antonio: *"I'm with Drew from the Truth Information Network. We're wondering why there's a blimp flying overhead at three in the morning. Drew, what do you wanna say about these surveillance blimps?"*

Drew: *"My experience has been that they usually have it out anytime there's a major event. But the only problem I've seen with this is they've had it out three days before and three days after. Why would they have it out three days before and after the event?"*

Antonio: *"This was the white Sanyo blimp, right?"*

Drew: *"It's the white blimp with the red Sanyo logo on both sides. We need to get people to be more aware of events that look strange like this in their towns. People just go about their daily lives and don't focus on anything important. People need to wake up and realize we no longer live in a free country. Strange shit happens every day, but people just don't notice it."*

***

Antonio: *"I told you a minute ago about my friend, whose teacher is a Freemason; this teacher took him to the Masonic Temple here in Detroit. I've heard that Detroit is the Masonic capital of the world.*

The Masonic Temple is evil as hell. My friend took pictures of the coffins and all their coded ritual books. He asked them, 'Okay, when do we get to see the evil shit?' At that point, the guy shot them an evil stare and kicked them out."

My friend's teacher told this Freemason, *"We have a charity. We do great things. Our charity is the Child Relocation Act."*

So, I'm thinking, *okay, what's that mean? Are you guys going to find someone's child and put a tracking chip in them? Or are you guys going to be the Satanic pedophiles we know you are? Shout out to Bush and all of his Satanic pedophile cronies."*

Drew: *"They're probably linked with Child Protective Services. So, whenever somebody has a complaint against you about your child, they can come and grab 'em. They'll take them away and then throw them into this country's "Abu Ghraib" foster system.*

I mean, they damage children. They send 'em into foster care, and they get treated worse than any child should ever be treated or put through. So that's probably what their little charity is doing."

***

Antonio: *"The blimp keeps circling over the stadium. Why would he be going over the stadium? The stadium has been abandoned since 1999. Unless the stadium is now a concentration camp, this could be a new FEMA camp."*

Drew: *"Try and get that verified. Yeah, find that out 'cause that'd be something I definitely need to know."*

Antonio: "I wish I had crystal clear footage of this like Jones had on Martial Law 9/11: Rise of the Police State.

The people trying to rule everything are scared. That's why they're constantly trying to push this bullshit down our throats.

If everything was going according to their plan, would they be doing this stuff? Would they be detaining people? Would we have concentration camps in this country?"

Drew: *"Everyone, you need to Google FEMA camps!"*

Antonio to the general audience: *"If you don't know about these FEMA detention camps...go to Google and search FEMA Detention Center. We have 600+ detention centers in the U.S. We have three in Michigan that I know of. Why do we have detention centers?*

They say that with the declassified Rex 84 program, detention centers will be used for illegal immigrants and in times of national security threats.

What about the amnesty bill they have on the books? Will they not be illegal immigrants anymore? So, who are these FEMA camps for if they're not considered illegal immigrants anymore?"

Drew: *"The Fema camps are for us. For American citizens."*

Antonio: *"Exactly! Us, being people that don't want to see our country go to hell in a handbasket!"*

Drew: *"They're predicting violent protests. With violent protests, they can claim you as an enemy combatant. Those FEMA camps are mass storage for enemy combatants."*

Antonio: *"Why is there a blimp flying overhead at this time of day? What the hell is so important about this city? We need to hold this government accountable for all the crap they're doing. Is there a way to find out who owns the blimp?"*

Drew: *"I would say go search on the internet to find some information."*

Antonio: *"I'm gonna try to find something. There's gotta be some information on the internet."*

***

As you can see, conspiracy theories drag people into a dark space mentally. I was totally convinced that satanic pedophiles had infiltrated the government.

Conspiracy theories wield immense power over people. More so when these people meet other conspiracy theorists on the internet.

Remember in chapter two when I said conspiracy theorists meeting each other validates their ideas? And it gives them purpose and meaning?

Here's a picture of me with other conspiracy theorists at our Conspiracy Theory Brew & View we did every Sunday.

Over the past few years, conspiracy theories have become more prominent. They're no longer the realm of the fringes on the internet.

This wouldn't be a problem except for the fact that conspiracy theories can radicalize a person.

There are real-world consequences to conspiracy theories running amok.

Some conspiracy theories seem harmless. We're talking about stuff like aliens, Bigfoot, etc.

But the fact of the matter is this—conspiracy theories have a tendency to pull people in. Hence the saying *"going deeper down the rabbit hole."*

Where it starts getting dangerous is the theories that claim shadow governments rule the world. Or even the QAnon theory that satanic pedophiles in Hollywood are feasting on children's blood.

While it's easy to mock that belief, it's stood the test of time.

"But QAnon isn't that old. What are you talking about?" a voice pipes up.

Sure, QAnon is relatively new. But the belief that satanic people are feasting on children's blood is thousands of years old.

Thousands of years ago, Jews were accused of killing Christian babies and drinking their blood in satanic rituals.

Whoever is behind QAnon knew it would be bad optics to blame the Jews once again. So, they took the high road. Or less of a low road I guess. They reframed it from "The Jewish problem" to "The satanic Hollywood pedophile problem," which was smart on their part. You can't tell a QAnon supporter they are anti-Semitic and racist against the Jews, even if the theories they're cranking out about are based on anti-Semitism.

Take the Jews, for example. They have been the target of conspiracy theories for thousands of years. The groundwork had been laid to allow Hitler to slaughter millions of Jews.

Could Hitler have shipped Jews off to camps without convincing people they were part of some global conspiracy to control everyone?

Not likely.

Hitler took people's long-held fears of the Jews and ran with them. The Nazi regime capitalized on those fears and created "The Big Lie."

The Big Lie turned Germans against the Jews and helped to justify the Holocaust.

Nazis believed there was an international Jewish conspiracy theory for world domination.

A common theme in Nazi propaganda is Jews started World War II and tried to destroy Germany. Nazi forces used this as justification to round Jews up and toss them in the camps. They framed it as self-defense.

Once this was set in motion? It became easy to justify the Holocaust. After all, the Nazis were simply trying to defend themselves against the Jews. At least, that's how they saw it.

Let's take a step back and look at the locus of control concept mentioned earlier. The Nazis were operating from an external locus of control. Deep down, they believed Jews were a nefarious force trying to control the outside world.

What if Hitler operated from an internal locus of control? Rather than seeing the Jews as a threat to Germany?

Hitler's manifesto, Mein Kampf, clearly indicates he operated from an external locus of control. He placed power in the hands of an outside force, the Jews, rather than take control of his own life.

Let's look at a couple of other examples of conspiracy theories bleeding over into the real world:

Trump's Big Lie

Trump was very vocal about the 2020 election being stolen. He repeated his Big Lie often.

The result? Thousands of Trumpers stormed the Capitol on January 6th, 2021.

***

QAnon drives people to murder

On September 11th, 2022, a Michigan QAnon supporter killed his wife and himself.

His daughter posted this message on a Reddit support group for family members of QAnon members. Imagine Al-Anon for family members of QAnon supporters.

"Yep. The internet ruined him. Growing up, my parents were extremely loving and happy people. I always had a special bond with both my parents.

In 2020 after Trump lost, my dad started going down the Q rabbit hole. He kept reading conspiracy theories about the stolen election, Trump, vaccines, etc. He always said he wanted to keep us safe and healthy.

It kept getting worse, and he verbally snapped at us a few times. Nothing physical, though. He never got physical with anybody.

Well, at around 4 a.m. on September 11th, he had an argument with my mother, and he decided to take our guns and shoot her, my dog, and my sister. My mother succumbed to her wounds, and my sister is in the hospital right now.

My dad also fired back at the cops, and they killed him.

I'm shocked, and I don't even know what to say.

Fuck you, QAnon. I hope the FBI tightens its grip on you and that your lackeys rot in prison (and hell) for poisoning so many people."

My guess? Her father was probably up in the early morning hours on September 11th, researching 9/11 conspiracy theories. Then one thing led to another and he spiraled into mania. Keep in mind this is just my own theory.

If you'd like to support the family and pay for medical bills, etc. here is the GoFundMe that the family setup. Either the link below or the QR code will redirect to the GoFundMe campaign.

www.escapingtherabbithole.com/gofundme

***

Anti-Vaxxers causing harm

On December 31st, 2020, a Wisconsin pharmacist spoiled over 500 doses of Moderna's COVID-19 vaccine.

Steven R. Brandenburg was given a three-year sentence for intentionally destroying the vaccines.

Steven admitted he knew if the vaccines weren't stored properly, they would be ineffective.

His actions alone could have killed people.

***

Sadly, on July 6th, 2018, two 12-month-old babies died after getting their MMR vaccines in Samoa. It wasn't the actual MMR vaccine that caused their deaths. Instead, the vaccine was prepared incorrectly. Two nurses mixed the MMR vaccine powder with an expired muscle relaxant.

After these two babies died, anti-vaxxers convinced people in Samoa that the vaccine caused the deaths. Samoa stopped its vaccination programs for ten months due to mounting public pressure.

Then in August 2019, a passenger infected with measles flew from New Zealand to Samoa. As a result of the vaccination program being stopped and the infected passenger, a full blown outbreak happened in October 2019.

Eighty-three kids died of measles from September 2019 to January 2020. The reason? All because anti-vaxxers convinced Samoa residents the vaccine killed those two babies.

This outbreak was in direct response to anti-vaxxers spreading misinformation.

***

And it goes without saying that the anti-vaxxers were out for blood during the COVID-19 pandemic. I mean "plandemic," according to those Facebook scholars. HAHA.

Hell, Anthony Fauci received death threats from these lunatics. Anti-vaxxers claimed that Anthony Fauci was just in it for the money. His yearly salary as of 2019 is only $417,608. I don't know about you, but no amount of money is worth it to me to endure death threats.

***

Alex Jones fanboi attempts to take down a pedophile ring

On December 4th, 2016, Edgar Maddison Welch fired three shots from his AR-15 at a pizza joint in Washington, D.C.

The reason? He was convinced that the pizza joint, Comet Ping Pong, was keeping child sex slaves held captive.

Edgar told the police he planned to investigate whether the conspiracy theory was true in person. If true, he planned on rescuing the children.

It's a safe bet that he operated from an external locus of control. He saw these "satanic pedophiles" as the most nefarious force in the world. At the same time, he wanted to be the hero that saved these children.

I could keep listing example after example, but you get the point. As you've just read, conspiracy theories have a **massive** impact worldwide.

For now, do yourself a favor. Take a deep breath, go for a walk, take a hot bath, etc. Make sure to take care of yourself.

In the next chapter, we're going to cover an uncomfortable topic. Any guess what we're going to cover?

Chapter 6
What's Your Motivation for Reading This book?

Here's an uncomfortable truth—this chapter is all about you. Yes, we're shining the spotlight on you. Not to attack you but rather to lift you up as the main person in any intervention with your loved one.

Before you can influence someone to change, you'll need to change.

"What do I need to change?"

For starters, you'll need to change how you communicate with them. This is often easier said than done.

In the following chapters, we'll cover specific strategies to pull someone out of conspiracy theories.

But before you get ahead of yourself, you'll need to know what you want to happen.

Sure, the end goal is to rescue your loved one from conspiracy theories.

You'll only be able to get so far. Your loved one needs to be open to change. This is the whole *"you can lead a horse to water"* thing.

To get them to take the leap of faith, you'll need to set some goals for yourself.

What do you want to happen?

"I don't want my loved one to get stuck in conspiracy theories."

Okay, fair enough. That is what you DON'T want to happen. But what do you WANT to happen?

"I don't want my loved one to..."

Stop right there for a second. Let me run a rather unusual scenario by you.

Picture this:

You're at a restaurant with a friend. You've had your menus for a few minutes, but something seems off. Your friend has a look of confusion and overwhelm plastered on their face.

When your server comes around to them, your friend looks nervous as hell.

"What can I get you?"

"Um... I don't want a hamburger."

"Okay. What do you want?"

"Well, for starters, I don't want a steak."

"Sure thing. There are plenty of other things to choose from. What do you want?"

"I don't want the fresh catch of the day either."

Your server looks confused. After all, it's such a simple and straightforward question:

"What do you want?"

"I don't want this, and I don't want that."

Your friend is thinking about the things they don't want. You tend to get more of what you focus on. By focusing on what you don't want, you'll remain stuck.

You see, our mind has a hard time processing a negative. To process a negative (not doing something for example), we need to focus on what we won't be doing.

For instance, don't think of a purple toy elephant. And definitely, whatever you do, don't think of a purple cow.

Try not to think of a purple cow tiptoeing through a field of freshly cut grass.

To not think of any of these, your mind has to first think about them.

Just know it's far better to focus on a positively framed outcome. In other words, having something happen versus something not happening.

To make your job easier, let's play a fun game.

I want you to make a list.

"A list of what?" you ask.

A list of all the things you DON'T want to happen regarding your loved one.

Use the blank lines underneath the examples below to create this list. Or get some paper and your favorite magic writing stick.

Example: *"I don't want to yell at my brother."*

Example: *"I don't want to get frustrated with my sister about conspiracy theories."*

Example: *"I don't want to engage with Mark about conspiracy theories."*

Example: *"I don't want to lose my temper with my loved one."*

Example: *"I don't want to lose my dad to QAnon."*

So bust out a list of all the things you don't want to happen.

_____

_____

_____

So far, so good. Now for the fun part!

Now I want you to write down what you WANT to happen. Having trouble at first? Look at the list you wrote down and work backward from there. It might end up being the opposite of what you wrote above.

Example: *"I don't want to get angry with my mom about QAnon."* → *"I want to be calm when talking to my mom about QAnon."*

Also, make these are things you can control directly. You can control your own behaviors, choices, and actions. You can't control anyone else.

Example: *"I want to remain empathetic with my loved one."*

Example: *"I want to remain curious with my loved one."*

Example: *"I want to see things from their perspective."*

Example: *"I want to show my loved one respect."*

Example: *"I want to respect my loved one's model of the world."*

_____

_____

_____

We're about to make some magic happen! But first, we have to make sure your goal/outcome is something you can control.

While you can't directly control what happens in the world, you can manage your behavior and choices. Your behaviors and choices can have an impact on your environment.

We're going to take you through an exercise known as WOOP. WOOP is the brainchild of German Psychologist, Gabriele Oettingen.

"WOOP, there it is!" you shout out in song and dance.

Stop it! Let's stay focused.

WOOP is an effective tool for hitting your goals/outcomes. It stands for Wish, Outcome, Obstacle, Plan. [1]

I'll describe the WOOP process below. I would like to suggest that you download the free WOOP app on either the play store or the Apple store. The APP guides you through the entire process.

For now, just pick one goal/wish. You can always tackle other goals with WOOP later.

---

[1] Rethinking Positive Thinking: Inside the New Science of Motivation, Gabriele Oettingen. pg 118

Wish: This is the goal you have in mind.

NOTE: You want to make your wish something you can control. Instead of *"I want them to listen to me,"* make it something you can control.

"I want to listen with compassion and curiosity," for example.

Write your wish below on the blank line (or on separate paper) in three to six words.

_____

_____

Outcome: What's the best possible result of achieving your goal? In other words, how would achieving this goal make you feel?

What would be the best thing about fulfilling this wish? How would fulfilling this wish make you feel?

In three to six words, write down the best possible outcome of achieving this wish:

_____

_____

Now take a few minutes to visualize fulfilling this wish. Close your eyes and imagine achieving this goal. Feel those good feelings in your body as you imagine fulfilling this wish.

Now that you've got some feel-good chemicals in your body, it's time to make them disappear.

"Wahh? I don't want to feel bad. Are you some sort of sick masochistic dominatrix or something?"

"Who me?" I say as I bat my eyelashes.

There's an excellent reason for this. Just follow along, and it'll make perfect sense.

Obstacle: This is the inner obstacle that is likely to trip you up later. Identify what it is in you that would prevent you from achieving this wish.

What internal struggle or obstacle would stand in your way of fulfilling this wish?

Below or on another piece of paper, write down in three to six words the inner obstacle or struggle:

_____

_____

*Example: If [**frustrated with brother**], then I will [**take three deep breaths**.]*

Write your If/then plan below (or on a separate piece of paper):

If _____, then I will _____

Next, close your eyes. Imagine being in a future situation where you will likely experience that internal struggle.

Repeat this if/then plan mentally while you imagine engaging in this new action/behavior. Mentally repeat this over and over. Repeat the mantra of *"If [obstacle] then I will [action]"* while you imagine engaging in that action.

I'd suggest repeating this if/then plan at least 15 to 20 times. Take as much time as you need.

There you have it! You've just completed your first WOOP.

"How will I know if it's worked?"

Great question! The best way to test this is in the real world. Meaning go to the situation that would have caused the old behavior/reaction to occur.

Here's a quick recap of the steps:

Wish: This is the goal you have in mind. Write this down in three to six words, or as close as you can get to that.

Outcome: What's the best possible result of achieving your goal? In other words, how would achieving this goal make you feel? Write this down in three to six words, or as close as you can get to that.

Then imagine fulfilling this wish and achieving that outcome as fully as possible.

Obstacle: Identify the inner struggle or obstacle preventing you from achieving this wish.

Jot this down in three to six words.

Then imagine this inner obstacle or struggle as fully as you can for a few minutes.

Plan: Identify the action/behavior you can take to overcome this obstacle.

Next, create an If/then plan with this action.

If *[inner obstacle]*, then I will *[action]*

Then imagine being in a future situation where you're likely to experience that inner obstacle. Slowly repeat the If/then plan in your head as you **imagine** engaging in that new behavior.

WOOP is a great science and evidence-based approach to changing your habits and behaviors.

I'd suggest getting the free WOOP app. Head over to the google play store or the Apple store. The app will guide you through the entire process.

Having trouble getting WOOP to work? Here are some great troubleshooting tips:

If the WOOP process doesn't work the first time around, look at your wish. Your wish needs to be as feasible and specific as possible. You want this wish to be challenging but doable. If it helps you can chunk it down into smaller steps/wishes.

The outcome needs to motivate you as well as leaving you feeling fulfilled. Make sure to visualize this outcome as clearly as possible.

For the obstacle, make sure it's an inner obstacle. Visualize it as clearly as possible in the third step.

The plan needs to be formulated as "*If [obstacle], then I will [action]*". This also needs to be an action you can pull off. If you don't have the necessary skills or resources, either work on getting those skills or resources. Or? Find another action that you can take.

Want to have me guide you through the WOOP process and make it easier to understand? Watch the free video at the link below:

www.escapingtherabbithole.com/woop

In the next chapter, we'll cover the three things you have in common with every conspiracy theorist. Can you guess what these three things are?

Chapter 7
My Conspiracy Theory Daze

Still guessing what three things you have in common with every conspiracy theorist?

You can stop guessing because I'll reveal it shortly.

"Oh god, quit teasing me! Why won't you just tell me already?"

For starters we need to look at my Conspiracy Theory Daze that was caused by these three things.

Conspiracy Theory Daze refers to two things.

It refers to the amnesia of my time spent as a conspiracy theorist. It also refers to the time I was actively involved in conspiracy theories.

This was roughly from 2002 to 2008—give or take a little bit of time.

Jesus, that's a huge chunk of time to devote to any one thing.

That time could have been spent far better.

"Can we get a cleanup on Aisle 3? We got a sensitive bitch tits crying over spilled milk."

Anyhow, I guess this book was written for two reasons:

1) To help you rescue your loved ones from QAnon and other conspiracies.

2) To help unpack my thought process at the time.

There is a simple explanation why I developed "amnesia" around that time. I'm not going to lie. It's an embarrassing part of my life. There's no way to cut around that. So naturally it's easy to block it out mentally.

We're about to dig into an interesting concept.

"Pray tell, what is this concept we're about to dive into?"

We'll get to this concept in just a bit. For now, let's take a quick detour.

Picture this:

I'm at a gorgeous restaurant soaking in the sunset over a Hawaiian beach. Sunlight is dancing and tiptoeing off the water.

Everything on the menu looks incredible.

Pumpkin patch ravioli, tender filet mignon with bacon butter. Dessert? A chocolate cake with exotic Tahitian vanilla whipped cream!

All the food is incredible. The sunset is sneaking out of view past the horizon. My belly is full.

Everything has been incredible up to this point. I should stop while I'm ahead.

But oh no, why would I do that?

After all, I'm 'Merican. You can't tell me what to do with my body. I have rights damn it! Here, shovel that chocolate cake into my mouth!

One bite in, and I spit it out. Imagine a perfect-looking chocolate cake with the flavor of nothing but baking soda! My taste buds were just assaulted.

We had been deceived!

Up to this point, the menu has been a good representation of what to expect.

Have you ever ordered something that sounded delicious on a menu only to be let down?

Was the menu lying to us? Not at all. The menu was a representation of what to expect. The nasty-tasting dessert was the reality.

There's a perfect explanation for this. It boils down to a concept known as:

The Map Is Not the Territory

We respond to our "maps" of reality rather than directly with reality itself. We are constantly making sense of the outside world with our five senses.

Two people can experience the same event, yet come out with wildly different perspectives of what happened. We've all been there before.

Think back to an experience you shared with someone where you had a difference of opinion of what happened.

Was it a different experience for each of you? Nope. The difference is how the event/experience was interpreted.

Philosopher and engineer Alfred Korzybski coined the phrase, *"The map is not the territory."*

Korzybski knew that humans tend to confuse models of reality with reality itself. A model can represent something but is not identical to the thing it represents.

Hence the phrase, "The map is not the territory." Or, in the case of the restaurant, "The menu is not the meal."

How we interpret something isn't identical to the actual thing. Take a map of the United States for example. This map represents the U.S. It's not actually the U.S.

Our minds create maps of reality to make sense of the world. Mental maps are our interpretation of reality, not reality itself.

Think of something you used to believe when you were a young kid.

Perhaps you believed that:

When you were little, a bearded man flew over your parents' house at night. Not all the time, but only one night a year.

And guess what? He managed to shimmy down your chimney. To top it off, he even left presents for you under a tree!

You can see where this is going.

If you were raised to believe in Santa Claus, then you had a specific "mental map" that Santa Claus fell into.

You might have even heard the pitter-patter of reindeer feet on the roof! It's amazing what the mind will do to convince you that something is real, or even that a belief is real.

This is good ole confirmation bias at play. If you're not familiar with confirmation bias, it's the tendency to search for, interpret, favor, and recall information that confirms or supports one's prior beliefs or values.

I jacked that definition straight from Wikipedia. Wait. Do you expect me to fact-check that? In a book about debunking conspiracy theories? Ha!

The irony is not lost on me.

85

You might have even created a wild fantasy or story about Santa flying around at night.

But something happened, and you discovered that Santa Claus wasn't rea...

Wait... I'm not going to spoil it for you.

These mental maps are full of shortcuts, almost like cheat codes. These maps help us navigate the world.

Imagine if we had to make a conscious decision every time we came up to a closed door. We would have to consciously pull up memories of us opening doors to know what to do.

That would overwhelm us before we even left our house.

Good luck driving without killing someone if you had to consciously think about it. Just imagine if you had to remember every single rule of driving.

"Seat belts, turn the car on, reverse, turn the wheel, drive forward."

That's overwhelming as hell. And you haven't even left your driveway!

What happens if you're barreling down the road with distractions all around you? Not to mention you have to think about hitting your brakes. And turn signals. There's no way you could pull this off every single day.

As we go through our life experiences, our minds develop maps based on these experiences.

Remember the question at the beginning of the chapter? The one about the three things you have in common with every conspiracy theorist? Let's take a look at those three things right now.

These three things are as follows:

Deletions, Distortions, and Generalizations

Deletions involve selectively paying attention to some aspects of our experience while we exclude other elements of our experience.

In hypnosis, there is something known as negative and positive hallucinations. This isn't a hallucination that a schizophrenic might have. Instead, it's a common occurrence we all experience.

A negative hallucination is when you don't see or hear something in your environment.

For Example: Have you ever gone to the fridge looking for ketchup, but you couldn't see it anywhere? No matter how much you look, it's not there. But it is.

And maybe you're looking high and low for your car keys, but they're on the table right in front of you.

A positive hallucination is seeing or hearing something in your environment that isn't there.

Ever heard your name being called? Then you realize no one is around? You may have seen a mouse or a cockroach out of the corner of your eye. Only to find out it's a figment of your imagination.

Distortion is when we mistake something for what it's not.

"The fact the local police force is running a domestic terror drill means they will cause a false flag shooting." Or something along those lines.

You can see how distortion plays out in a conspiracy theorist's mind. They tend to distort a lot of stuff. This isn't to say that we are immune to these filters.

"My wife smiling at her co-worker means she's having an affair." Maybe it does, maybe it doesn't.

Conspiracy theorists are prone to cognitive distortions, especially if they're not challenged.

I experienced an example of distortion while doing my nightly walk about two hours ago. I'm walking down the street and coming up to someone sitting on the curb. He's wearing a dark hoodie.

"Okay, they look like they might be a shady character. I should cross the street."

As I get closer, I look right and get the shock of my life!

It was a couple of garbage bags piled on top of each other.

Crisis averted. I didn't have to bust out any of my ninja skills. By ninja skills, I mean hiding. Haha.

What might have happened if I didn't realize it was just a pile of black garbage bags?

I might have changed my walking routine tomorrow. A story would have been woven in my head that said, *"You need to cross the street when you get up to this corner."*

But it would have been a false story. Would I have known that unless something corrected this distortion in my mind? Not likely.

The third rule our brains make are generalizations.

Generalizations are conclusions we've come to based on one or more experiences.

"I should cross the street if I see someone in a black hoodie."

"All men are dogs."

"All mass shootings are false flag operations designed to take our guns away."

Generalizations are true for us until they aren't. It doesn't mean they fit in with actual reality itself. Just that they are accurate until they're challenged.

Our generalizations aren't necessarily a bad thing. They help us to navigate the world. For instance, all cars operate much in the same way. Well, except for the recent introduction of self-driving electric cars.

We've made up generalizations about how cars operate. If we weren't able to do this, we'd be having mass casualties on the road every day.

I've got another story from my conspiracy theory daze to illustrate the power of updating mental maps.

Let's take a trip back to 2005:

I'm firmly in the clutches of Alex Jones. I'm eating up all the garbage he's spewing out.

I'm heading up to the bar I work at. I'm there to help run the Conspiracy Theory Brew & View we've been running for two years. We drink beer and watch conspiracy "documentaries" to fight back against the Illuminati and the New World Order. Chuckles. Like we could even do anything against a government armed with high-powered firearms.

Oh, we also snorted cocaine.

"It's not the cocaine making me paranoid. It's the government," I would say jokingly as I rubbed my nose.

Newsflash: it was the coke making me more paranoid if you didn't catch on by now.

A taxi drops me off in front of the bar I work at. As I walk up to the bar, confusion rolls in like a thick cloud.

There are no lights on. An entire bar, usually jammed with people, is a ghost town. It's as if there was never any action in there to begin with.

As I walk toward the front door, confusion crashes in on me. I see a letter posted on the front door.

"This establishment has been closed by the Michigan government."

Then it hits me like a ton of bricks. I've been waking people up to the New World Order every Sunday for two years, and now the Illuminati and NWO are trying to shut us up. Those tyrannical bastards want to keep us silent.

I'm standing in front of the bar feeling waves of panic and paranoia creep in. My hands start trembling and my body is going numb. I'm mumbling to myself, looking unhinged as if I have an invisible Bluetooth in my ear.

Paranoia creeps in on me like an old man shuffling over and tapping his cane.

Clickity clackity, someone has gone whackity.

"If they know we were exposing them, how soon before they come in and take us away to the FEMA camps?"

Panic rushes through my veins while my heart is pounding and cracking against my ribcage.

Thud…thud…thud…

It's as if I can hear my heart crashing against my chest.

"What am I going to do if they find me?"

I manage to rush back to my parents' house without getting caught.

Hours go by before I hear from my co-worker who ran the movie nights with me.

"So Johnny didn't pay his taxes. That's why we got shut down."

Looking back, I know the bar owner wasn't running a tight ship. But my brain skipped over that important detail.

And the letter on the front door of the bar?

This was an example of distortion. If you recall, distortion is when we mistake something for what it's not.

This letter was symbolic to me. It represented the New World Order trying to shut us down. Rather than stopping and looking at the letter, my mind blew things out of proportion.

Guess what?

Had I stopped and looked at the letter, I would have likely seen that it was from the Department of Taxation, or whatever government agency the notice was from.

I can't remember what was on that sign. This is another example of my brain deleting something from my experience that would contradict my beliefs.

I had a generalization until that day: *"Anything bad that happens is because of the New World Order."*

Up until that point, this generalization was solid. This new evidence showed me a local government agency shut the business down temporarily. It wasn't the New World Order.

Come to think of it, this was just another of the many experiences where my mental maps had been challenged and updated. Eventually, this gave me enough leverage to jump ship from crazy town.

I didn't see the bar owner not paying taxes as the reason for getting the bar shut down.

Anyhow, the good news is these rules and mental maps can be updated.

How?

By challenging your loved one's mental maps while coming from a place of curiosity, compassion, understanding, and love.

You don't have to believe their mental maps but just respect they have a particular way of "making sense" of the world. By accepting this and respecting their model of the world, it's easier to influence them to change.

You'll need to remain flexible regarding their model of the world. In the next chapter, I'll walk you through a powerful exercise to help you come from a place of curiosity, compassion, understanding, and love.

You've made some incredible progress so far. Also realize we're just getting the ball rolling.

You should get your hands on another great book: *How to Have Impossible Conversations* by Peter Boghossian and James Lindsay.

Peter Boghossian has a great system known as Street Epistemology. Street Epistemology is a way of helping people update their mental maps via specific questions.

In the chapter: **"Conspiracy Converting Questions,"** I'll include some strategies from his book. And my own unique take on some of them.

Next chapter you'll sink your teeth into a technique that will help you to remain calm and neutral when talking to your loved one. No matter how much they're trying to push your buttons. See you there!

Chapter 8
How to keep calm when talking to your loved one

If you're ever been in a heated argument with a conspiracy theorist you're going to love this chapter. Here's why:

Every single person is unique. Every one of us. We've all had unique experiences, both good and bad. We've all had our ups and downs.

Anything and everything that has happened on our journey has impacted us in one way or another. Respect that. You don't need to respect someone's beliefs or even hold the same ideas.

It can be hard to get through to someone, especially if they're on the opposite end of the political spectrum.

The good news is it's possible.

Bad news? It may be uncomfortable at first. It requires you to change how you communicate with your loved one.

You should respect that your loved one has their own beliefs as well as the right to those beliefs and their own model of the world.

NOTE: This doesn't mean you have to respect their views. Just respect that they're entitled to their own ideas.

It doesn't matter how disgusting you think those beliefs are. It's your job to set aside judgment. We'll discuss how to pull this feat off in a bit.

Come across as judgmental, and you've lost them. You'll want to come from a place of curiosity, love, and compassion. I promise you'll get a much better result as soon as you do this. That said, the techniques in this chapter are more geared toward you and your personal development.

"Why? I'm not the one with the proble—"

Hey, sorry to interrupt you there. You're going to get a lot out of this chapter. On top of helping you communicate better, you'll also get more control over your emotions.

Imagine how great getting control over those runaway emotio—

"LISTEN! I TOLD YOU ALREADY! I'M NOT THE ONE WITH THE PROBLEM!"

You swing your hand back, palm open ready to strike.

"I AM IN PERFECT CONTROL OF MY EMOTIO…."

Then it dawns on you. You realize that you've let your emotions get the better of you at times. Some of those times are when you talk to your loved one.

Deep down, you know it just adds fuel to the fire.

But the truth is it can be hard to control our emotions at times. Soon you'll be like a master monk in control of your feelings. It's best to communicate with them with the same level of respect you'd want in return.

Yes, I'm aware conspiracy theorists can be vile. After all, Alex Jones' followers were prepared to kill some pizza parlor pedophiles.

Try saying pizza parlor pedophiles three times fast!

Actually, don't do that. Legend has it you'll open a portal, and MAGA grifter Matt Gaetz will show up with his 17-year-old girlfriend.

When stepping into a situation with a certain "energy," the other person can feel it.

It's simple body language and humans feed off each other. Jesus, I realize that's a poor choice of words, especially when conspiracy theorists think Democrats get high by drinking baby blood.

That's such a silly idea. Babies don't taste good.

I warned you in the disclaimer that I have a dark sense of humor. My humor is pretty crazy. Well, not compared to your loved one ¯_(ツ)_/¯

Ready to become ~~a Jedi master of your emotions~~ a less whiny and emotional bitch tit? Especially when dealing with your conspiracy addicted loved one?

First, I have a question for you:

Have you ever seen a political protest erupt into flames?

I'll bet $10 you've seen a protest go up in flames on TV over the past few years. Unless you've had your eyes closed that is.

Two sides getting in each other's faces, shouting and screaming, calling each other vile names.

Because that's how you change someone's mind, call them names, attack their beliefs and values. Kidding. Don't do that.

Get a load of this crazy story:

It's March 15th, 2007. White supremacist Richard Spencer rallies the troops. (By troops, I mean a small crowd barely packing a tiny room).

A protest erupts outside, and Randy Furniss, a lone skinhead looking the part, is trapped in the crowd.

The crowd rushes in, and Aaron Courtney, an African American activist, moves within inches of his face.

"Why do you hate me?" Aaron asks him.

What Aaron did next shocks the crowd. Aaron reaches out to Randy and embraces him in a hug, showering him with love instead of raining punches on him.

"I…I don't know," Randy muttered.

"I could've hit him. I could've hurt him. But something in me said, 'You know what? He just needs love,'" Aaron Courtney later said.

The neo-Nazi is stunned and thrown off balance. His mental map probably tells him black people act like thugs toward white people.

And when it didn't happen? He was shocked. For a brief moment his defenses were let down.

Did this completely change Randy Furniss? Who knows? Maybe, maybe not. My guess is it didn't completely change him, but that's not the point.

"What's the point then if it didn't make a radical change?"

Maybe it didn't completely change him. But it got the ball rolling. It might take a few experiences to change deeply ingrained beliefs.

You'll want to approach changing your loved one's beliefs the way you would at a restaurant serving elephant. One bite at a time.

Moral of the story?

Fire up the chainsaw and get to work on chopping up that elephant, into itty-bitty pieces. Metaphorically speaking of course.

chef's kiss

This experience helped to alter Randy's mental map—his "rule book" of how black people are supposed to act.

Sometimes all it takes is one-off events to radically transform long-held beliefs.

Have you ever been involved in a heated argument with someone trying to get your point across?

No matter how hard you try, you can't seem to see things eye to eye. Much less come close to the same understanding or follow their logic.

What if you were TRULY curious about where they're coming from? Or, God forbid, were compassionate about where they're coming from?

Listen closely:

The most flexible person in any situation wins.

"The definition of insanity is doing the same thing over and over and expecting different results." - Albert Einstein.

Ever feel like you're beating your head against a brick wall? You keep trying to knock some sense into your loved one. You barrage them with facts.

QUIT DOING THAT.

Conspiracy theorists' beliefs are insulated from facts.

You need to adopt a better more flexible approach. The person with the most flexibility and choices wins in any situation.

Think about it like this—when you're in an emotional situation, you often get tripped up because you only see one option.

After you take a breather and look at the situation from a bird's-eye view, you often see more choices. This can feel very liberating.

Imagine you're in an intense argument with no way out. You walk away for a moment to get a breather.

Does this mean you let them win the argument? Nope, not at all. You've controlled the situation by being flexible and exercising choice.

Sounds easy, doesn't it? Well it's not. Not unless you use these two tools:

1. Specific questions to foster empathy and compassion with your loved one.
2. The Circle of Flexibility

Let's take a moment and dive into both of these tools.

Specific questions to foster empathy and compassion with your loved one:

These are questions you'll ask yourself to further foster empathy and compassion for them.

As an experiment, I'll encourage you to try on two questions for size. Just ask them internally and see how they shift your perspective.

Imagine you're with your loved one, and they want to talk about QAnon or some other conspiracy theory.

First, ask yourself the question below and just sit with whatever comes up for a few moments.

"What is wrong with them? Why do they believe in these stupid conspiracy theories?"

Take a few moments to sit with how that question makes you feel.

Now shake those feelings off to get to a neutral baseline.

Now ask yourself the question below and compare how each question impacts you differently:

"I'm curious where they're coming from. What might they be getting out of conspiracy theories?"

Like before, take a few moments to sit with how that question makes you feel.

Next, try asking yourself some of these questions below. Make a note of which ones resonate the most with you. Ditch the rest.

"How can I help them see another perspective?"

"What has to be true in their model of the world for them to believe in this conspiracy theory?"

"What has to be true in their model of the world to believe in conspiracy theories?"

"How can I maintain my empathy while talking to X?"

"How can I maintain my curiosity while talking to X?"

"What do I find most curious about X's belief in conspiracy theories?"

"What is some aspect of their model of the world that I agree with?"

"What is some aspect of this person's model of the world that I respect?"

"What is some aspect of this person's beliefs that I respect?"

"What is some part of their experience that I respect?"

"What I do respect about this person's model of the world is?"

You don't need every question. Hell, you might only have to use one or two. Use your best judgment. Take a few minutes to identify the question(s) that resonate most with you.

Up next we have the...

The Circle of Flexibility:

Go grab a pen and some paper. Or just a pen if you're going to write in the blank lines coming up. Seriously, go and do that. I'll wait here.

(My momma didn't raise no fool. I know you didn't budge from your seat. Seriously, take a minute and get your favorite magic writing stick. Nothing beats putting pen to paper. Go on, git!)

Okay, good.

Next, think about the top two to three emotional states you feel when you're feeling emotionally flexible.

Emotional and behavioral flexibility often contain emotions such as curiosity, creativity, compassion, empathy, feeling grounded, etc.

If it helps, close your eyes and *imagine* you can see yourself acting and behaving with a lot of behavioral and emotional flexibility.

I'd like to suggest including curiosity and compassion at the very least. Use the blank lines below and write the top two to three emotional states you associate with emotional flexibility:

_____

_____

_____

Now that you've got those answers, we're ready for action. Head on over to the website link below to do the exercise:

www.escapingtherabbithole.com/flexible

WARNING: Don't continue reading until you've gone through the video on the link above. The rest of this won't make sense at all.

Now that you've created this emotional trigger let's discuss how to use it.

Think of a time when you need to be more flexible. Maybe talking to a loved one who is knee-deep in conspiratorial thinking. Perhaps you're talking to them face to face.

Rate your emotional inflexibility (call it anger, frustration, anxiety, whatever it may be) on a scale of 0 to 10. 0 being the most emotionally flexible and 10 being the worst (most frustrated, angry, etc.)

1. Stand outside this "circle of flexibility" — if this doesn't make sense, go watch the video at www.escapingtherabbithole.com/flexible

2. Think about a context where you want to be more flexible with your loved one. Close your eyes and imagine being in this context.

3. Take a moment to play this situation out in your mind. Imagine everything you will see and hear in this context. Step into the circle of flexibility whenever you feel any negative emotions/emotional inflexibility coming up. This may come in the form of the urge to correct your loved one, if you're feeling angry, frustrated, etc.

4. As you feel these good feelings flooding back into your body, *imagine* acting and behaving in a more flexible manner with your loved one.

Also, imagine them responding and behaving to you differently as a result.

5. After doing this for a few moments, step back out of the circle.

6. Repeat Steps 1 to 5 a few times.

This process is beautiful because you're stepping in and out of emotional states. You're stepping from the negative suck emotion into the flexible feeling in the circle and then back out.

You're teaching your mind that you can step into a flexible way of being whenever you want.

NOTE: To make this technique even more powerful, ask yourself one of the curiosity questions you picked earlier in this chapter.

When feeling good in this imaginary circle, ask yourself one of those questions to direct your experience and imagination.

Watch the video at the link below to make it easier for yourself. I'll guide you through the entire process:

www.escapingtherabbithole.com/flexible

How do you think my life would have changed if someone had been curious about my beliefs rather than attacking me?

Let's look at the story from the last chapter. The one where I thought the New World Order got the bar shut down.

What if a friend had been truly curious about where I was coming from? Had someone remained curious, empathetic, and compassionate, they could have kept me from spiraling out of control.

Better yet? What if I had applied these techniques myself? I likely would have walked up to the bar with a much different mindset.

"Hmm, that's odd. I wonder why the doors are closed? What are the possible reasons for this?"

Being curious would have made a massive difference in my mindset. I would have moved from an external to an internal locus of control.

Quick refresher: your locus of control is where you put your focus and your control/power. Are you driving the car, or are you a passenger? If you're the latter, things just happen to you on this journey called life.

You're on an incredible journey. You've already taken a huge first step in helping your loved one and society. Together we can fight back against the conspiracy peddlers. They make money off the fears and insecurities of your loved one.

From this point on, it's us versus them. Remember, when I say "we," it's the sane Republicans and Democrats. Let's not let the fear mongers win.

In the next chapter we'll uncover two essential skills you need when talking to your loved one. Can you guess what the two skills are?

Chapter 9
Two Skills You Need to Rescue Conspiracy Theorists

Out of the many skills in this book, we're about to cover two of the most important ones. These two skills allow you to connect with your loved one. Without these two skills, you're dead in the water.

"So, what are these skills?"

The first essential skills is the ability to build and maintain rapport with your loved one. Any clue what the second essential skill is? The answer might surprise you. We'll reveal the second skill right after this story:

I'm sitting at a bar in Downtown Detroit. It's probably 2006 or 2007.

It's a Sunday night, one of our Conspiracy Theory Brew & View nights. Earlier in the book, I mentioned how we used to run a movie night with conspiracy movies because you should always talk politics and religion in a bar. Kidding of course.

One night the bartender was pushing back on the claims Alex Jones made in the video we were watching. But, rather than have a civil conversation, it started to get heated.

Since I devoted so much of my time and energy to exposing people to the Illuminati, I felt like he was attacking my core identity.

If you directly attack someone's beliefs and ideas, it's like telling them, *"You're not a good person."*

Needless to say, I shut down. At that moment, I felt like he was a sheeple that would never "wake up." So I slapped a label on him via the ad hominem logical fallacy. If you're not aware, ad hominem's are when you attack someone's character rather than their argument.

I built a wall so I wouldn't have to start doubting my beliefs.

Why'd this happen?

We only watched conspiracy movies that fed into our preexisting beliefs. When you're part of a group that believes a particular way, you tend to think everyone feels that way, or at least should.

You may even become fanatical about converting people to your worldview.

What happens if someone pushes back and tries to change your beliefs? If you're like most people, you simply shut down.

This can manifest in different ways for people. You might feel anxiety in your chest. Perhaps you have a disoriented feeling, like being confused. And on and on.

Humans can only handle so much discomfort for so long. We will do everything in our power to feel normal again:

- shutting down a conversation
- label someone with a personal attack rather than attacking their argument
- using a habit to feel normal again—smoking a cigarette, drinking alcohol, stress eating, etc.

Let's look at the first essential skill—rapport. Rapport, if you're not aware, is when two or more people are in a close and harmonious relationship and sympathetic to each other's interests. It involves mutual understanding, trust, and respect.

I'm about to make a prediction, and that is there are two possible scenarios at play here:

1) You used to have rapport with your loved one, which has been damaged.

Or

2) You never had a good relationship with your loved one, and rapport could have been better.

With this being said, you can always work to improve your rapport moving forward. One of the most common ways taught to therapists and coaches is Matching and Mirroring. This technique is where you match and mirror someone's verbal and nonverbal communication:

- adopting a similar posture to them
- speaking at the same speed and volume as them
- matching and mirroring their gestures
- adjusting your rate of breathing to match theirs

When people are in rapport with each other, they automatically match and mirror each other. So there's no need for them to consciously adjust their body language, rate of speech, mannerisms, etc.

While matching and mirroring can be effective, you risk coming off as mimicking them. A much better approach is to have a genuine interest in this person. Behave as if you actually care for them.

"What if I can't stand them?"

Then you need to work on yourself first. Talk to a therapist if you need to. Use the exercises in Chapter 8. Or schedule a 20-minute no-cost strategy call to discover how I can help you communicate with your loved one from a place of compassion, empathy, and love.

Use the link below to schedule your 20-minute no-cost strategy call:

www.escapingtherabbithole.com/call

On the other hand, if you don't have any significant reason to avoid building rapport with your loved one, read on.

Rapport Technique #1: The Instant Rapport Switch

This is an easy tool to use. You'll access feelings of what it's like to be in rapport with someone. Next, you're going to imagine feeling this way with your loved one.

I'll describe the technique below. To make it easier for you to implement, I've added a video guide at the link below. The video takes a hands-on approach and will guide you through the entire process.

www.escapingtherabbithole.com/rapport

Step 1. Think of a person you love hanging out with. Someone that you have a great time with when you're hanging out.

Step 2. Recall a memory where you had a great time together.

Step 3. Close your eyes and go back to this memory. Remember everything you could see, hear, and feel at the time. Allow the pleasant feelings to flood back into your body (feelings of connection, rapport, compassion, etc.)

Step 4. Allow everything you see and hear in this memory to become more intense; allow the colors to get brighter and allow the sounds to get louder. As you do this, you'll notice the pleasant feelings getting stronger.

Step 5. When the feelings are nice and intense, gently squeeze your right or left hand into a fist. Hold your fist for a few seconds while you can still feel these feelings intensely. If the feelings start fading loosen your fist up.

Step 6. Shake off any of these pleasant feelings that might still be lingering.

Next, gently squeeze your hand into a fist and notice how these feelings flood back into your body automatically.

You've just successfully created an emotional trigger you can activate anytime you want! Repeat this exercise a few times as needed to strengthen this emotional trigger.

Bonus tip: use a different memory every time you do this exercise with the person you have great rapport/connection with. You can also use memories where you've felt love and compassion.

Once again, to make things way easier for you go and watch the video at the link below. It will guide you through the entire process. It will be much easier for you to do this.

www.escapingtherabbithole.com/rapport

Here's how to use this rapport trigger:

Close your eyes and imagine you're talking to your conspiracy addicted loved one. Then gently squeeze your hand and allow these pleasant feelings to flood back into your body.

Next, imagine being in rapport with your loved one while you feel these feelings of connection.

By activating this "rapport trigger" and imagining being in rapport with your loved one, you're telling your subconscious how you want to behave and react in the future.

Another way to use this rapport trigger is by gently squeezing your hand while talking to your loved one in real-time. Just allow the feelings of connection to flood back into your body while talking to them.

If you're losing rapport, gently squeeze your hand into a fist again and allow these feelings to come back.

I've made a video for you to simplify the process. The video does all the heavy lifting and guides you through the entire process. In fact, the video has a more in-depth process that will help you get the most bang for your buck.

To make things easier on yourself watch the video at the link below:

www.escapingtherabbithole.com/rapport

Ready for the second essential skill? Let's get the show on the road...

One of the best skills to have is the ability to listen. Listening is quickly becoming a lost art form.

When we're firing on all cylinders, it clouds our judgment. Imagine being able to get through to someone a lot easier. This is a real possibility when you just <u>shut up and listen to them.</u>

You'll show your loved one that you listened to their concerns and care for them.

Remember, it's easier to catch flies with honey. Or however that saying goes.

We're about to discover two techniques to open your ears as well as keep your lips glued for a little while—just long enough to let your loved one speak their mind.

Does this sound familiar?

You're talking to a conspiracy theorist, and it's getting heated. With every claim they shoot out, you're chomping at the bit. Before they finish talking, you're already thinking about what to say.

Your mind is caught up in your own thoughts. Rather than being present with them you're already looking to barrage them with facts. (As an interesting side note, don't bring facts to the table. Facts give conspiracy theorists a reason to put up their defenses.)

Yes, it can be painful to listen to someone knee-deep in conspiracy theories, even more so if it's as bad as QAnon for instance.

Think you wouldn't be able to keep your cool while your loved one spews conspiracy garbage?

Look no further than Daryl Davis. Daryl is a blues guitar player from Chicago.

"What can I learn from a blues guitar player?"

First of all, you can learn how to deradicalize KKK members, which is a big deal. Want to know the kicker?

Daryl Davis is black.

Yep, a black man de-robed a bunch of Klan members. He didn't do it by force or coercion. If a black man can talk to Klan members and convince them to give up their Klan memberships, surely you can put your loved one on the right path, right?

Being able to listen to people is what helped Daryl to de-robe over 200 Klan members. On the surface, this is significant. But looking even deeper, it's nothing short of a miracle!

Think of it like this:

A Klansman's robe is very important to them. These robes are very symbolic to them. It represents a rich history to them. It also represents specific values to a KKK member.

These robes represent patriotism, security for their families, and belonging to a secret society dating back to 1865.

In short, their whole identity and way of life is tied to their involvement with the Klan.

117

Take their robes away and they'll feel naked. The fact that Daryl convinced Klan members to WILLINGLY hand their robes to a BLACK MAN speaks volumes to the power of listening to people.

Listening to someone is as simple as that. You just have to do it. If you have any urges to interrupt your loved one, you'll need to rein those urges in.

Active Listening Technique #1

If you're struggling to interrupt them, you should use the WOOP technique in Chapter 6. Remember you can download the free WOOP app. Go download it if you haven't done so already. The app makes using WOOP really easy.

Here's a quick refresher:

Wish: This is the goal you have in mind. Write this down in three to six words or as close as you can get to that. Since this section is all about listening, I'd suggest choosing a goal/wish along listening to your loved one.

For example, "Listen to my brother."

_____

_____

Outcome: What's the best possible outcome of achieving your goal? In other words, how would achieving this goal make you feel? Write this down in three to six words below (or on a separate piece of paper).

_____

_____

Next, imagine fulfilling this wish and achieving that outcome as fully as possible. Close your eyes and take a few moments to fully imagine this.

Obstacle: Identify the inner struggle or obstacle preventing you from achieving this wish.

Jot this down in three to six words below (or on a separate piece of paper).

_____

_____

Next, imagine this inner obstacle or struggle as fully as you can for a few minutes.

Plan: Time to create a conditional plan. Think of an action/behavior you can take to overcome this obstacle out in the wild. Taking a deep breath, going for a walk, meditating, etc.

Next, create an If/then plan with this action.

The formula is If [inner obstacle], then I will [action]

Example: If [**feeling frustrated**]_, then I will_ [**take three deep breaths**._]

Write your If/then plan below (or on a separate piece of paper):

If _____, then I will _____

Next, close your eyes. Imagine being in a future situation where you will likely experience that internal struggle.

Repeat this if/then plan mentally while you imagine engaging in this new action/behavior. Mentally repeat this over and over. Repeat the mantra of *"If [obstacle] then I will [action]"* while you imagine engaging in that action.

I'd suggest repeating this if/then plan at least 15 to 20 times. Take as much time as you need.

Want to have me guide you through the WOOP process and make it easier to understand? Watch the free video at the link below:

www.escapingtherabbithole.com/woop

Let's look at the next technique…

Active Listening Technique # 2: The L.I.S.P Speech Pattern

This is a simple technique to use. It's a framework for showing your loved one you're listening.

L.I.S.P. stands for:

- **Listen** and let them talk without interrupting them.
- **Identify** their position or belief.
- **State** their position back to them.

- **Paint** them in a favorable light.

Step 1. Listen and let them talk without interrupting them.

This is exactly like it sounds. Let them talk and just listen. Don't plan on your next rebuttal. Just shut up and listen to them.

Step 2. Identify their position or belief.

Keep your ears open for anything that sounds like a belief or a position they're holding.

Step 3. State their position back to them.

"Just to make sure I'm not misrepresenting you, you believe X, right?"

If they say no, ask them to clarify their position.

"So you believe X, right?"

"So your position is X, right?"

Step 4. Paint them in a favorable light.

"You seem like a person who can engage in civil and productive conversations."

"You seem like a person who is open-minded, and you can have civil conversations."

"You seem like a person who can keep their cool and have a civil conversation."

"You seem like a person who is easy to talk to."

If they disagree with whatever quality you place on them, you'll want to abandon this technique. Or ask them what qualities they think they possess.

I'd suggest writing out a couple of these to keep tucked away in your back pocket for when you need them.

In the next chapter, we'll cover what I call *"conspiracy converting questions."* These Socratic-style questions help loosen your loved one's beliefs in conspiracy theories. Rather than work on their beliefs directly, some of these questions help them realize how they came to believe what they believe.

Some of these questions were borrowed from Peter Boghossian and James Lindsay's book **How To Have Impossible Conversations**. I'd like to suggest you grab that book. It's a great compliment to this book.

One of the things this book and *How To Have Impossible Conversations* have in common is mentioning how you need to come from a place of love, curiosity, and compassion. The difference is my book has techniques to help you do this.

If you're still struggling with communicating without getting emotionally riled up, I have to first ask you if you did all of the exercises in chapter 6 and 8?

What if you could change your loved one's minds by asking a series of powerful questions? The next chapter has a handful of questions you can use to shift damn near anyone's mind. I'll walk you through the entire process. Let's push forward!

Chapter 10
Conspiracy Converting Questions

What if you could rescue your loved one from conspiracy theories by asking a series of sneaky, yet effective questions?

This chapter is all about opening a line of communication with questions. As you'll soon discover, questions are the backbone of influencing pretty much anyone.

For example, a salesperson won't get anywhere without asking a few questions.

Before I get ahead of myself, let's dive into another story about the power of questions:

It's August 2007. I'm walking down the street to my parents' house. A shady-looking white van with "Google" printed on the side pulls up next to me. Sure, it has Google plastered on the outside, but how can I be certain?

This van is slowly driving down the street, matching my pace. I pause and take a step, and the van follows my lead.

"Why are they following me?" I think to myself.

Then it hit me that this was no regular van. This is one of the vans tasked with mapping out street views. But deep down something feels off.

I stop in front of my parents' house, and the van follows suit. My heart's pounding.

I sneak a peek over my right shoulder as I take a drag from my cigarette.

"Why are they taking pictures of me?" My mind was racing with various possibilities:

"Maybe they're aware of our movie nights in the bar where we're exposing the New World Order?"

"Maybe they know I'm exposing them?"

"Maybe it's because I supported Ed and Elaine Brown during the government raid on their property over income taxes!?!?!?"

And on and on. We're talking a merry-go-round of batshit crazy.

Later my suspicions proved to be true. Well, partly. You see, I went and checked Google Maps and saw my picture on the street view. I could see myself peering over at the van.

I used this as evidence that they were trying to track us 9/11 Truthers/Patriots. Yes, this sounds crazy as I write this.

Let's look at the question I asked myself:

"Why are they taking pictures of me?"

It's an open-ended question. Open-ended questions encourage us to think more deeply about what we're being asked (as well as what we ask ourselves). These types of questions allow us to provide more thought-out responses.

These kinds of questions are also great for shaping beliefs. Take *"Why does no one love me?"* That question will provoke your unconscious to dish up an answer.

Closed-ended questions require virtually no conscious thought. We answer Yes or No, and we go about our day.

Let's look at the question again: *"Why are they taking pictures of me?"*

If I had asked myself, *"Are they taking pictures of me?"* I would have gotten an entirely different answer.

It would have been a Yes or a No. A closed-ended question is like coming to a full stop at a stop sign. With closed-ended questions, there's no room to keep going.

When you ask someone an open-ended question, they're more than likely going to give you an answer, especially if you're coming from a place of compassion and curiosity. Someone could have easily reframed my belief about why Google was taking pictures by asking me:

"What else could that mean?"

"What are the other possible reasons for taking pictures?"

"What are some other simpler explanations you haven't looked at yet for them taking pictures?"

The kind of questions we ask ourselves and others influence behaviors and thoughts.

I will list some specific questions you can start playing around with. I've borrowed these questions from various places. Some of these are from the hypnosis/coaching world, especially the scaling questions (i.e., *"On a scale of 0 to 10"* questions).

Another great book you should grab is Peter Boghossian and James Lindsay's *How to Have Impossible Conversations*. They have some great strategies in that book to help people come to new beliefs.

How to set up a conversation

You should make it easy for your loved one to have productive conversations with you.

First off, explain how they could convince you to join their side if they could more clearly explain a conspiracy theory and how they came to believe it.

"As an open-minded person who is good at having civil conversations, you could get a lot more people to join your side if you were to explain how you came to believe X... and I'm not following how you got to that conclusion... could you help me fill in the blanks and connect the dots?"

I'd recommend practicing reading the statement above out loud as many times as you need. In fact, you should also write it a few times to really wire it in.

The more you practice saying it aloud or writing it down, the more it will flow off your tongue.

What makes that statement so magical? For starters, it places your loved one in a particular role. You're painting them with a broad brush when you say, *"As an open-minded person who is good at having civil conversations..."* [2]

---

[2] How To Have Impossible Conversations – A Very Practical Guide, Peter Boghossian & James Lindsay pg 139-144

We all like to think of ourselves as good people. When someone else acknowledges a positive trait or quality in us, we try to live up to that. This statement also implies that they didn't always have this particular belief in question.

And last but not least, you're opening them up to discovering how they came to believe what they believe.

In addition to this, we've got the...

Unread Library Effect

You know the vocal know-it-all conspiracy types? The Unread Library effect describes them perfectly. [3]

People often think they have a broad knowledge of a subject because they have access to information such as books on the subject. Or because they know a person who is an expert on the topic.

Having access to knowledge on a subject causes us to believe something is correct. It's like believing something is correct because the information we access confirms it, even if we've never read the information.

We're fooling ourselves if we haven't read the books and absorbed the information.

[3] How To Have Impossible Conversations – A Very Practical Guide, Peter Boghossian & James Lindsay pgs 36-39

When we try to explain a subject we thought we had more knowledge about, we start to doubt what we actually know. It causes us to see the gaps in our understanding.

The bigger the gap between what someone thinks they know and what they actually know, the more of a know-it-all they come across as. You can politely ask someone to explain their belief or position clearly and in detail.

Before you attempt to shift their belief, get a baseline for where they're at by asking a scaling question:

"How confident are you on a scale of 1 to 10 that X... with 10 being the most confident and 1 being not confident at all?" [4]

Example: *"How confident are you on a scale of 1 to 10 that satanic pedophiles run the planet... with 10 being the most confident and 1 being not confident at all?"*

If they choose any number lower than 10, follow up with *"Why didn't you pick a higher number?"* They're expecting you to ask why they didn't pick a lower number. Asking them why they didn't pick a higher number causes them to introduce doubt.

If they answer with a 10, try asking them:

"It sounds like you're pretty convinced this is real. I'm curious. What would have to happen for it to become a 9 or an 8?"

---

[4] How To Have Impossible Conversations – A Very Practical Guide, Peter Boghossian & James Lindsay pgs 86-89

Or trying asking them:

"I'm at about a 6 on the 1 to 10 scale of believing X. I'm kind of lost how you got to such a high number. Can you please walk me through how to get there?"

"Personally, I'm at about a 6 on a scale of 1 to 10. Could you help me discover how I could get to an 8 or a 9? How would I go about doing that?"

Here are some additional questions to loosen up their beliefs and expose the Unread Library fallacy:

"And how do you know that?"

"Why do you think this is true?"

"When did you first realize this was true?"

"When did you first believe this was true?"

"What would have to happen for this to be untrue?"

"Is there any way this could be proven to be untrue, and if so, how?"

"If you wanted to convince your younger self who didn't believe in this yet, how would you do that?"

"When did you first start forming this belief?"

"Under what conditions could this belief be untrue?" [5]

---

[5] How To Have Impossible Conversations – A Very Practical Guide, Peter Boghossian & James Lindsay pgs 105

"In what ways could this belief be untrue?"

"What are some other possible answers you haven't thought of yet?"

"I'm a little confused about how you got to the idea that X. Can you help catch me up to speed?"

Another possibility for them choosing a high number or acting like there is no evidence that could prove the belief to be false:

It's a strong indicator that the belief is formed around their morals. A moral belief is binary—it's a yes or a no. In their mind, someone would be either good or bad if they didn't believe in a particular belief. [6]

To root out if it's a moral view, ask them:

"Would someone not believing this belief make them a good or bad person?"

"What would you say about a person who did not believe this?"

Another way to discover if it's a moral issue is to ask questions like these:

"What would no longer believing X say about you?"

"What would no longer believing X mean about you?"

Up next we have this hypnotic question...

---

[6] How To Have Impossible Conversations – A Very Practical Guide, Peter Boghossian & James Lindsay pg 117

"Has it ever occurred to you...."

The beauty of asking if something has occurred to someone is that it gets them to think about it. It's a gentle way to get them to ponder an idea.

"Has it ever occurred to you that the government is too inept and stupid to pull off a widespread conspiracy such as blah blah blah?"

If they answer along the lines of *"No"* or *"No, it hasn't occurred to me,"* you can follow up with, *"Oh, so it hasn't occurred to you yet?"*

"Has it ever occurred to you that the New World Order wants you addicted to your phone and as many social media apps as possible?"

"Has it ever occurred to you that foreign governments might be spreading vaccine misinformation on social media to weaken our country from within?"

I'm sure you can think of a couple of ways to help shift your loved one's beliefs with *"Has it ever occurred to you..."* Try to think of ways to apply this to introduce doubt in your loved one.

"Has it ever occurred to you that Alex Jones might be a CIA asset?"

"Has it ever occurred to you that the deep state might have invented QAnon to make conspiracy theorists look stupid?" This might be a fun one to play around with.

"Has it ever occurred to you that Democrats might have started QAnon to make conspiracy theorists look stupid?"

"Has it ever occurred to you that NASA might have started the flat Earth theories to make conspiracy theorists look stupid?"

"Has it ever occurred to you that social media companies want to get you hooked on their products and turn you into a liberal with no self-control?"

"Has it ever occurred to you that Democrats might have created QAnon to discredit Trump because Democrats can't be trusted?"

And it doesn't stop there...

"Wouldn't you agree...?"

Wouldn't you agree that adding *"Wouldn't you agree"* to the front of a sentence makes it easier to agree with?

You don't want to go overboard and abuse this language pattern. Just sprinkle it in here and there. If you use it too much your loved one will catch on.

Example: *"Wouldn't you agree we should protect kids at all costs?"*

"Wouldn't you agree the Democrats might have created QAnon to discredit Trump?"

"Wouldn't you agree we should be able to have a civil conversation?"

"Wouldn't you agree we should be able to have a civil conversation about how to keep children safe from pedophiles?"

"Wouldn't you agree we should be able to have a civil conversation about how to keep children safe from satanic pedophiles?"

Only you'll know how to best use this in your conversations. You should look back at your conversations with your loved one to know how to best use this pattern.

133

If it helps, write a few examples to wire this pattern into your conversations. In fact, I'd recommend writing multiple examples of each of these patterns. You can wire them into your conversations more easily and automatically by writing them out and practicing saying them aloud.

But wait, there's one more...

"If X, then Y, fair enough?"

This is a brilliant language pattern to get agreement. I've used this with a lot of success in sales.

This is a cause-and-effect language pattern. It comes across as simple logic. If X happens, then Y will naturally happen. It's like a natural progression. Then you tag on *"fair enough?"*

When done correctly, you'll get an automatic agreement from your loved one—from a verbal "Yes" to a head nod.

Example: *"If your purpose in life is to keep people safe, and you can do this by volunteering at the local homeless shelter, I'd love to see you do this. Fair enough?"*

Example: *"If your purpose in life is to protect your family, then we should look at a few possible solutions. Fair enough?"*

Example: *"If you discover some aspect of this conspiracy isn't real, then you can reevaluate your belief. Fair enough?"*

Example: *"If you prove this conspiracy theory to be untrue, then I'd love to see you update your position on this. Fair enough?"*

Example: *"If your mission in the world is to feel safe, then we should look at a few ways you can do this more easily. Fair enough?"*

Example: *"If your purpose in life is to save the planet, then we should look at a few possible ways you can do this easily without tipping off the deep state. Fair enough?"*

Once again, I suggest writing out a bunch of examples using this pattern. The more examples you write out, the more easily you will be able to use this in your conversations with your loved one.

Here's a bonus for ya...

The Agreement Frame Redirect

Ok this one isn't a question. Rather it's a powerful way to steer a conversation in any direction that you want.

Warning: do not over use this. It will come across as very manipulative. Use it sparingly.

Have you ever had someone disagree with you before? Right off the bat, they've shut down the conversation. A better approach is to agree with some aspect of their argument/belief.

"I agree X..."

"I agree we should punish pedophiles..."

"I agree that some politicians are shady..."

"I agree it looks like social media platforms censor Republicans..."

"I agree you think satanic pedophiles are running the planet..."

135

"I respect that you think x"

"I respect that you believe x"

Next, you'll want to steer the conversation to a more productive outcome:

"And I'd like to add that the issue might not be X... rather Y... which means we should Z."

So the entire thing looks something like this:

"I agree X...and I'd like to add that the issue might not be X, rather Y... which means we should Z."

Example: *"I agree you think satanic pedophiles are running the planet... and I'd like to add that the issue might not be satanic pedophiles running the planet...the issue might be whether or not we have proper laws in place to prosecute these pedophiles...which means we should look at what laws are in place to take care of this."*

Example: *"I agree it looks like social media platforms censor Republicans...and I'd like to add that the issue might not be social media platforms censoring Republicans. The real issue at hand might be social media platforms are causing people to become addicted to their programs so they can control them...which means we should look at ways to fight back against social media from controlling our lives."* (**note**: this could be a perfect way to introduce the idea of taking a break from social media. Chapter 12 covers a technique for this.)

Example: *"I agree some politicians are shady, and I'd like to add that the issue might not be shady politicians. Rather, the real issue might be what steps can be taken to address shady politicians. Which means we should look at what specific laws can be used if a politician gets busted doing shady stuff."*

Example: *"I respect you believe the Deep State is pulling the strings, and I'd like to add that the issue might not be Deep State pulling the strings. Rather the real issue might be whether or not we have proper laws in place to prevent this from happening in the first place. Which means we should look at what specific laws would prevent this from happening."*

To get the most out of this chapter, write out a bunch of these questions over and over. Practice saying these in the mirror until they become second nature.

So there you go. You now have a good set of questions to help shift your loved one's beliefs.

If you like what you've read in this book so far, I'd love for you to leave me an honest review on Amazon. Fair enough?

See what I did there ;)

You can use the link below to leave a review. It redirects to the Amazon page for this book you're reading.

www.escapingtherabbithole.com/amazon

Thanks for the review!

Chapter 11
The Hidden Benefits Technique

Has it ever occurred to you that your loved one gets an emotional benefit from engaging in conspiracy theories?

Now what if I told you that you can help rescue them by uncovering this emotional benefit?

Believe it or not, but it's true.

The good news is this chapter reveals how to do this. We're talking step-by-step.

The concept we're about to dance with in this chapter might not make sense at first, but deep down, you'll instinctively "get it."

You'll see how this concept affects damn near all human behavior. This goes for your loved one and you. We're talking everyone.

The basic idea is that there is an emotional payoff to engaging in behaviors. This goes for thoughts as well.

There's a concept that states, *"Behind every behavior, there is a positive intention."* Don't confuse this to mean a behavior is positive; it can be negative and destructive, yet still have a positive intention.

Also, remember that a person isn't their behavior. Behaviors are just something they do. It can often be hard for people to drop negative habits and behaviors because they internally label themselves as the behavior.

If you've ever heard someone say, *"I'm a smoker,"* this is a prime example. They're confusing a behavior with an identity. I'll bet dollars to doughnuts you've never heard someone say, *"I'm a driver."* Not unless they drive for a job that is.

Let me tell you a quick story that illustrates this point.

About six or seven years ago, I was in the back of a gasoline-powered hunk of metal. We're flying down a bumpy dirt road at breakneck speeds. Every bump threatens to launch us off the road to our death.

The floor of the car is littered with a woman's mutilated body parts. Terror sets in.

"Why are we tossing her out of the car??!!?" I scream inside my head.

At this point, I snapped awake from this horrific nightmare—a nightmare that wasn't a one-off. This recurring nightmare was only half of it.

On top of these horrific dreams, I was terrified of the dark. Imagine a 37-year-old panic-stricken man darting for his room when he flicked off the bathroom light.

Or God forbid if the shower curtain was closed:

"What if there's a serial killer on the other side of the curtain?!!??"

My game plan was to shut off the light, dart to my bedroom, and jump in bed; the whole time feeling like someone was behind me, causing my skin to curl.

It made no logical sense that I was terrified and thought a serial killer was hiding behind the shower curtain. Like he couldn't come up with a better plan than sneaking into my apartment and waiting a few hours for me to go to the bathroom.

Yeah, that sounds silly now.

One day I told my mom about these nightmares that have always plagued me. She broke some horrible news to me.

When I was about six years old, our neighbor's girlfriend was killed by his ex-girlfriend. It was pretty bad from the sounds of it. We're talking about being kidnapped and mutilated.

By now, you might be making connections as to why I thought there was a serial killer behind the curtain. Or even why I kept having those recurring nightmares.

Finally, everything made sense! My subconscious was trying to keep me from getting killed. My subconscious had a mission; to keep me safe.

And guess what happened when I got an insight into what was fueling my lifelong fears?

Jack shit. My fears kept haunting me.

So having insight into why someone has a fear or a problematic behavior isn't necessarily a good thing. Sure, I finally knew why I had these nightmares and lifelong fears. Just knowing my neighbor's girlfriend being kidnapped was the cause didn't do anything to resolve my issues.

In fact, sometimes having insight into why you are the way you are can do more harm than good. You're basically telling yourself a story of why you are the way you are. A story that can reinforce the same bad habits or stuck patterns.

It wasn't until I tried a meditative process known as Core Transformation that I got any relief.

Picture this. I went from a 37-year-old man terrified of the dark and my own shadow to being unable to bring back any of that fear.

It's been seven years since I resolved that fear. I cannot bring back any of those panicked feelings for the life of me.

As an aside, I'd recommend getting a copy of the *Core Transformation* book if you want to eliminate any fears, negative thoughts, or behaviors.

It's been a lifesaver for my clients and myself.

If you'd like to discover how Core Transformation can help you to improve your life or your relationship with your loved one, jump over to the link below and schedule your no-cost 20-minute strategy call with me:

www.escapingtherabbithole.com/call

Core transformation is a "parts therapy" technique. It works under the premise that our feelings, thoughts, and behaviors are controlled by unconscious "parts" of us. You can see these parts as our mini-selves that control our behaviors.

With parts therapy, you imagine having a conversation with the parts of you responsible for problematic behaviors.

Next, you simply ask this part something such as: *"What do you want?"* or *"What are you trying to do for me?"* or *"What purpose or function do you serve?"*

When I used core transformation to transform the fears of our neighbor's girlfriend being killed, the answer I got back from an inner part of me was:

"I want to keep you safe from getting hurt."

I finally hit pay dirt!

Which is incredible when you think of it like this; this part wasn't trying to hurt me by causing fear or giving me nightmares.

It was trying to keep me from being kidnapped and murdered.

What started as a "negative behavior" and something that felt destructive turned out to be an excellent resource. Have you ever engaged in a negative behavior even though you didn't want to? You keep getting wrapped up in that behavior no matter what you try.

It's as if you felt compelled to continue engaging in this behavior. You may have had some negative thoughts that kept bouncing around.

Who else wants a taste of Parts Therapy in action?

If so, think of a negative feeling, behavior, or thought you've been dealing with. Don't go for something that has a lot of emotional turmoil wound up behind it. Just think of something relatively benign—something that is more of an annoyance.

1) Close your eyes and imagine you're in a situation where you engaged in this negative behavior, feeling, or thought.

2) Scan your body and notice any feelings or sensations that let you realize, *"This is the part of me responsible for this."*

3) Get a sense of where this part would reside in or around your body.

4) Take a few moments to **thank this part** for being here. Thank this part for doing something positive for you up until this point even if you're not sure what this positive thing is.

5) Ask this part one of these questions:

"What do you want for me?"

143

"What are you trying to do for me?"

"What purpose or function do you serve?"

Take as much time as you need with the last step. Don't try to rush the answer. You're not trying to strong-arm or reason an answer out, you're looking to have an imaginative dialog with your subconscious.

The most critical step is to thank that part and welcome it.

You probably won't be surprised by the answer you get. When we get a taste of "parts therapy" in action, we realize what these behaviors have been doing for us all along.

You want this part to feel like you genuinely want to communicate with it, but not from a judgmental place, rather from a place of compassion and genuine interest in what this part has to share with you.

Also, take your time with this little thought experiment.

This is to give you a taste of the concept *"Behind every behavior, there is a positive intention."*

To make things easier for you, I created a video where I'll guide you through the entire process. And I've added a nice bonus in the video to help you find relief from this thing that has been a minor annoyance to you:

www.escapingtherabbithole.com/parts

I have helped quite a few clients transform self-destructive behaviors with parts therapy processes (such as core transformation I mentioned earlier).

The parts therapy I've done with my clients and myself boils down to a variation of these questions:

"What does this part of you want?"

"What does doing X do for you?"

Where X is the behavior, negative feeling, or thought.

"What does doing X allow you to feel or experience?"

"What's important to you about X?"

Here are some examples of how it usually goes:

Me: "What does smoking a cigarette allow you to feel or experience?"

Client: "It allows me to relax and connect with other smokers."

The positive intention for them comes down to relaxation and connection with others.

Me: "What does telling yourself that you're stupid do for you?"

Client: "It helps to keep me from making a stupid mistake."

Any guesses what the positive intention behind that one is? It can help protect this person from looking foolish for example. Ultimately it boils down to protection.

Me: "What's important to you about quitting smoking?"

145

Client: "I want to be healthy and be around for my kids."

When a person answers questions along those lines, it reveals a lot of information about them.

First and foremost, you'll discover what their values are.

Next time you're talking to your loved one, ask them questions like:

"What does researching conspiracy theories do for you?"

"What does researching conspiracy theories allow you to feel or experience?"

"What does exposing the Deep State do for you?"

"What does exposing the Deep State allow you to feel or experience?

You'll know when you've hit their emotional hot buttons; watch as they light up emotionally. Their posture and breathing can shift. Uncovering the values that really move them might take a few rounds.

When you're on the right track, dig deeper.

"Can you tell me more about X?"

Example *"Can you tell me more about this safety?"*

Get them to talk about those values.

You can use these values later to open a discussion; where you can influence them to shift their locus of control from external to internal. Hell, get them to share stories where they've experienced those values.

(Remember that the locus of control is where someone places control of their life. Are they a passenger, or are they driving the car?)

Another way you can help your loved one is to find other habits and behaviors that allow them to experience their values.

"If there was an easier way to experience X, you'd be interested in finding out, right?"

"If a healthy hobby or habit allowed you to experience X, what do you think it might be?"

Have them list hobbies, behaviors, and actions that allow them to experience their values. After they've got a list of healthier alternatives, it's just a matter of doing these things.

And that's not all. Next up is the:

Hidden Benefits Technique

Another process you can use is what I call the hidden benefits technique. It's a simple self-hypnosis/meditation technique from my colleague, Dr. Richard Nongard. [7]

For this to work, you'll first need to uncover what exposing conspiracies does for them.

---

[7] The Self-Hypnosis Solution – Step-By-Step Methods and Scripts to Create Profound Change and Lifelong Results, Dr. Richard Nongard pg 54

You'll want to discover what kind of emotional benefit/payoff they get.

You can ask, *"What does doing X do for you emotionally?"* Or you can ask, *"What does doing X allow you to feel or experience emotionally?"* or *"What's important to you about x?"*

Example *"What does researching conspiracy theories do for you emotionally?"*

Example *"What does researching conspiracy theories allow you to feel or experience emotionally?"*

Example *"What's important to you about exposing the New World Order?"*

Note: You can gently poke and prod to get to their core values/desires with these questions:

"Can you tell me more about X?"

"What does this allow you to feel and or experience?"

That's it! Now you just help them create an affirmation around this core emotional benefit:

Example: *"I Am Feeling Safe."*

Example: *"I Am Feeling Grounded."*

Example: *"I Am Feeling Centered."*

Step 1. Have them get into a comfortable position and close their eyes.

Step 3. Inhale for a count of four.

Step 4. Exhale for a count of six.

Step 5. State the affirmation: *"I am feeling X."*

It's essential that they really *step into* this feeling.

Step 6. Repeat eight times.

"And? Is that it?"

Yes, it's really that simple! This technique works by creating a shortcut in their mind; to give them the emotional benefit/payoff they usually get from conspiracy theories.

Before they know it, their mind finds out it can jump straight to this emotional reward.

Let's turn back to the story you read earlier. What could have happened if I had applied either technique in this chapter?

For starters, I could have asked myself:

"What does thinking there is a serial killer behind my shower curtain do for me?"

My first instinct would be "to scare me." The outcome was that I was scared. But what was churning below the surface? It was trying to protect me and make me feel safe.

Possible hobbies, behaviors, and actions that could have satisfied *"protecting me"* are:

Meditation, exercising, bulking up, going to a therapist, etc.

What if I applied the hidden benefits technique?

Here's how it could have played out:

Let's ask myself, *"What's important to me about stopping the New World Order?"* or something like, *"What does exposing the NWO and the Illuminati do for me?"*

My first instinct is "to keep people safe". And feel safe myself. Safety as a theme has been a strong motivator in my life.

Geez, I wonder if feeling unsafe because of our neighbor's girlfriend being killed had anything to do with it?

You probably caught on faster than I did. Hell, it took like thirty-two years for me to put two and two together. Never said I was the smurtest in the bunch. And yes, I spelled it smurtest.

Next, I could have whipped up a list of habits and actions to satisfy this emotional need for safety:

- Deep breathing
- mindfulness meditation such as Leaves on a Stream
- swimming
- walking daily (which I've done a LOT of lately)
- and on and on

The possibilities are endless.

From here, it's just a matter of implementing those things. Focusing on something that helped others feel safe would have significantly improved my life at the time.

Luckily, I cleared up most of my issues with core transformation and other modalities.

If your loved one shows a genuine interest in changing but needs help to start implementing this stuff, jump to Chapter 14. You can use the simple techniques in that chapter to help them wire in these new habits.

You've just been exposed to a powerful technique. Give yourself a huge pat on the back. You deserve it.

Yes, this journey can be dark and daunting at times; but realize that your loved one is simply lost. What is the best thing you can do? Hold up a light to show them the way out.

Here's a sneak preview of the next chapter:

You're going to discover a simple way to help your loved one break their addiction to conspiracy theories. This includes breaking addictions to social media; Truth Social, Reddit, Facebook, Telegram, Gab, and on and on.

Chapter 12
Conspiracy Theory Craving Buster

What if I told you there was a scientifically proven way to break your loved one's addiction to conspiracy theories?

As crazy as it sounds, it's completely true.

In this chapter, you're getting up close and personal with how to detox someone from dangerous conspiracy theories. Better yet, you'll learn how to help them resist the temptation of conspiracy theories.

Imagine how much better off your loved one will be without QAnon and other destructive conspiracy theories dominating their life.

I can say with 100 percent confidence that conspiracy theorists get almost all of their information from the internet. This goes without saying.

In fact, the internet is almost solely responsible for the spread of this trash. Well, not directly responsible.

Conspiracy theorists still have to spread this misinformation. Obvious, I know. Watch any conspiracy theorist on a digital device; evolutionary biology is at play.

It's no random chance they've been wired to respond to misinformation. The mere act of picking up a phone gets their juices flowin'. Phones have been engineered to be impossible to put down.

Digital crack. Catnip for conspiracy theorists.

Social media companies have spent BILLIONS to make their platforms impossible to resist. Websites have also been developed and tweaked to get us addicted.

"Hey, I get that. What can I do to stop my loved one from overdosing on QAnon?"

Great question! We'll cover a scientifically proven technique in a bit. But first, pull up for a story:

It's April 2020. The world has been flung into a zombie apocalypse.

But I'm blissfully unaware. I've managed to avoid Facebook entirely. Call me old-fashioned, but I want some peace and quiet. I did miss Facebook at times. But not enough to tank my mental health.

Then it began.

I got the itch to *just check Facebook for five minutes.*

As soon as I opened Facebook, massive panic attacks started hitting me from every angle. I came back to Facebook during the HEIGHT of a global pandemic that millions of Americans wrote off as fake news.

Not the smartest thing I've ever done. But I've got at least another fifty years of dumb mistakes ahead of me. So I'm ahead of the curve by my logic.

I'd comment on a conspiracy-rich Facebook post and put my phone down.

"Did that QAnon moron reply?"

Facebook was causing me so much emotional turmoil. Yet I couldn't turn away. It was like watching a bad accident about to take place.

Like gawking at two gas-powered hunks of metal barreling down the road and kissing at the lips. No matter how often I told myself I wouldn't open Facebook, I got sucked back into the action.

"I know! I'll just delete the app from my phone!" I told myself over and over.

A few days passed before I buckled under the pressure. I'd start taking sneak peeks at Facebook on my laptop.

Ever catch a glimpse of someone addicted to their phone? Picture this—a lab rat meth monkey smashing buttons to get more dope dropped into their cage. As soon as a conspiracy theorist gets wrapped up in the internet, all bets are off.

The reason for this? A psychological principle known as "operant conditioning."

Operant conditioning is modifying behavior by attaching a positive or negative reinforcement. What's the easiest way to wrap your mind around it? With dog training.

Example: You tell a dog to sit and then show them how to do it.

Then when you tell them to sit and they actually do it? You give them praise and positive reinforcement.

Post a funny meme on Facebook for example. People come out of the woodwork and start commenting. Maybe they like and share the post also.

A roller coaster of dopamine. Wheeee!

God forbid someone shares your post! The gods of acceptance have bestowed glory upon thee! A feedback loop has been set up.

It looks a little something like this:

Post on Facebook → People respond → Dopamine → Post on Facebook

Rinse, wash, and repeat.

Social media companies have engineered their platforms to get you hooked. After a few repetitions your brain is hooked.

Before you know it, you're slamming buttons like a lab rat meth monkey. Make no bones about it, you're the product.

Now for the good news:

An addiction to social media can be broken in as little as 5 minutes a day. I know this sounds incredible, but bear with me because you're about to get the inside scoop.

Introducing a little-known strategy called Urge Surfing:

What's Urge Surfing?

That is exactly what the title says. An urge comes up, and you don't do anything. You sit there in the presence of the thing that causes the desire. Just sit there and allow the feelings to come and go.

Sorry if you thought I was going to drag some ancient wisdom down from the mountaintop that was buried for thousands of years.

Urge surfing is simple as hell. So simple a lab rat meth monkey could pull it off. Well, in between banging buttons and performing stupid tricks for humans.

With urge surfing, you expose yourself to the addictive thing; your phone, social media apps, website, etc.

"And? What's next?"

Nothing. Just sit there you weirdo. Resist acting on the urges to interact with the thing in front of you. Allow the cravings to come and go.

The result? You're rewiring the patterns in your brain. Simply put, you're short cutting your brain's reward system. Your brain learns *A craving doesn't mean you have to act on it.*

How to break addictions to conspiracy theories on the internet:

Step 1. Identify what delivery system of conspiracy theories your loved one is addicted to (specific apps, websites, social media, etc.)

Step 2. Set a timer for five minutes.

Step 3. Have them open the device they use to consume information (phone, desktop, laptop, tablet, etc.)

Step 4. Next, have them select the thing they're addicted to. (Truth Social, Facebook, Reddit, website, etc.)

Step 5. Start the timer for five minutes. Have them look at the thing they're addicted to without interacting with or touching their device.

Step 6. Tell them to breathe through the urges as they come and go. Deep breaths can help to push the cravings along even faster.

You could even turn it into a friendly competition. Got a problem getting stuck on your phone? Why not join in?

Both of you can sit there resisting the urge to pick up your phone, tablet, laptop, etc.

Want to up the ante? Place some money on the line. No one likes to think they're addicted to something. Use this to your advantage. Tell them you think they're addicted to their phone and can't set it down for ten minutes.

When they tell you they're not addicted, bet them $5 they can't leave their phone alone. People generally don't want to think of themselves as an addict. We like to think we're always in control. So use that to your advantage.

If they say, *"I'm not addicted. I can put the phone down anytime I want,"* play devil's advocate:

"Ok, whatever you say."

If they agree, ask them what app they use the most. Then explain how to do urge surfing.

NOTE: Is your loved one not ready to use this technique? This is perfectly fine. You can always circle the wagon later and introduce it to them again.

They can make this even more exciting by using the Habitica role-playing game app on their phone. Every time they do a round of urge surfing, they can win points, gold, etc., in the Habitica app. If they are a gamer, this app is a perfect fit. It uses gamification to help you hit your goals.

Every time they do a successful round of urge surfing they can win points in the game.

Here's a quick tip: Once they show interest in using this technique or any technique in this book, run them through the methods in Chapter 14, *"How to Motivate a Conspiracy Theorist to Change."*

How could I have kept the pandemic from keeping me glued to my phone?

For starters, I could have made a list of the apps that kept drawing me back in:

Facebook and Reddit in my case.

Next, it would've fired up Facebook on my phone. Then I'd set a five-minute timer.

And then? I'd just sit there and breathe deeply in and out whenever an urge or craving strikes.

Nothing more and nothing less. Seriously, give this technique a go yourself.

Don't have a problem with getting stuck on your phone? Use it to change your relationship with other things you crave such as sugary snacks.

With that being said, I'm glad you made it through this chapter. The fact that you've made it this far means you're dedicated to pulling your loved one back from the brink of madness.

That's the best you can do for now. Show them you care for them.

"What's in store for me in the next chapter?"

Glad you asked. You're going to discover how to help your loved one detach from intrusive thoughts. You know the ones we're talking about; the paranoid and anxious thoughts that they just can't seem to shake.

See you in the next chapter!

Chapter 13
How to Stop Paranoid and Anxious Thoughts

Does this sound familiar to you? You're watching your loved one, or another conspiracy theorist slip into madness.

Day by day they go deeper down the rabbit hole. At first some of their thoughts might seem plausible, but a little "interesting".

But before you know it? They're so far off the deep end.

It's obvious to you they are becoming increasingly more paranoid in their thoughts. They're racked with panic and anxiety.

Okay, now we're cooking. By now you're probably aware that anxious and paranoid thoughts are pivotal to conspiracy theories.

This chapter is all about how to let go of anxious and intrusive thoughts. Some of the best solutions I've come across are cognitive defusion exercises from ACT; which is short for Acceptance and Commitment Therapy.

ACT has great techniques to wrangle in negative thoughts. You know which ones we're talking about. They're scurrying across your mind kicking up dust and other nasties.

When we have negative thoughts, our first instinct is to dive into the deep end of the pool. Before we know it, we're drowning in these negative thoughts.

One of the best ways to control anxious and paranoid thoughts is by giving up.

"Giving up? Why would I tell my loved one who's on the brink of madness to give up?!!?"

Yes, you read that right! Let me clear up any confusion. We're not talking about giving up and tossing in the towel; more like giving up fighting with these thoughts.

When you battle against negative thoughts, isn't that like fighting with yourself? After all, you generated those thoughts. It's almost like saying:

"The part of me causing these negative thoughts is no good."

Guess what happens next? Those negative thoughts push back even more. Even if you win one of these battles, you still lose. A much better approach is a hands-off approach.

"A hands-off approach? Go on…"

Since you asked so kindly, let's tear into this. Right after I drop another story for you.

It's 2007, and I'm jumping back and forth between manic episodes. Highs and lows brought on by booze, conspiracies, and cocaine.

"Oh, but the coke isn't making me paranoid. It's the government!" I preached. Here's a hint—it was definitely the coke making me more paranoid.

And to make matters worse?

Every time I fired up Myspace, conspiracies assaulted me left and right. It felt like one emotional face plant after another. Reading one of these posts would send me hurdling down a never-ending train of obsessive thoughts.

"Well, looks like I'm not getting any sleep tonight. I've gotta crack the case!"

My thoughts would be bouncing off the walls—chemtrails, FEMA camps, satanic pedophiles, etc.

You know how overwhelming this can be if you've ever been caught up in a train of negative or obsessive thoughts.

I'm sure you've seen the impact of obsessive or negative thoughts on your loved one. Watching someone slip into madness and not having a solution is frustrating.

Since our minds generate these thoughts, we easily identify with them. These thoughts seem real to us and are core to our identity.

There's a reason why lots of negative thoughts start with *"I am"* or *"I"*:

"I'm *a loser.*"

"I'm *a wreck.*"

"I'm *a fat ass.*"

"I'm *part of the resistance against the New World Order.*"

"I'm *a patriot.*"

"I'm *a freedom-loving patriot.*"

"I'm *a freedom-loving American!*"

Not every negative or obsessive thought your loved one has will be an identity-level thought.

It can be an obsessive thought such as *"Joe Biden is a satanic pedophile."* This is just an example. These intrusive thoughts don't have to start with *"I am" or "I."*

We identify with the statements we say to ourselves. Since our mind create these thoughts, we start believing them. Conspiracy theorists need to unhook from their anxious and obsessive thoughts.

"But how can they unhook from these thoughts??"

It sounds simple. It's not, unless you...

Get your hands on <u>this</u> secret weapon

"What's the secret weapon?"

The secret weapon is cognitive defusion. Cognitive defusion is the ability to see thoughts for what they are:

Thoughts. Nothing more and nothing less.

Have you ever experienced having a creative or groundbreaking thought? But then it vanished?

No matter what you did, you couldn't pull it back into the bone dome resting on your shoulders. That's head for some of you humorless people. Come on, catch up.

Where did those thoughts go? The truth of the matter is you let them go. Sure, this was an accident, but the fact remains the same. You unhooked yourself from the thought and simply let it go.

The key to cognitive defusion is to be aware of your thoughts rather than getting caught up in them or even buying into them.

It can be a simple yet revolutionary idea. We don't have to buy into OR act on our thoughts. As an extreme example—how many times in history have the "loose with reality" folks claimed, *"The voices made me do it!"*

Unfortunately, those people might have some severe mental illness going on. This is just to illustrate that our thoughts can be VERY persuasive.

Here is my favorite cognitive defusion exercise. I'll describe the process as if you're running through it. You can always explain this process to your loved one. Or download a guided meditation MP3 by going to this link:

www.escapingtherabbithole.com/act

Leaves On a Stream Cognitive Defusion Exercise

1. Sit in a comfortable position and close your eyes.

2. Imagine you're sitting next to a softly flowing stream with leaves floating on the water.

Pause for a few seconds to imagine this

3. For the next few minutes, take each thought that enters your mind and place it on a leaf. Just allow it to float by. Do this with each thought. It doesn't matter if the thoughts are pleasurable, painful, or neutral.

Even if you have positive or enthusiastic thoughts, place them on a leaf and let them float by.

4. If your thoughts stop for a few moments, continue to watch the stream.

Sooner or later, your thoughts may start up again. If this happens, place the thoughts on the leaves floating by.

5. Let the stream flow at its own pace.

Don't try to speed it up and rush your thoughts along. You're not trying to get the leaves to rush along or "get rid" of your thoughts. You're allowing them to come and go at their own pace.

6. If your mind says, *"This is dumb," "I'm bored,"* or *"I'm not doing this right,"* place those thoughts on the leaves and let them pass.

7. If a leaf gets stuck, allow it to hang around until it's ready to float by. If the thought comes up again, watch it float by another time.

8. If a difficult or painful feeling arises, simply acknowledge it.

Say to yourself, *"I notice myself having a feeling of boredom,"* or whatever it is you're feeling. Imagine placing that thought or feeling on a leaf and allow it to float along.

9. Occasionally your thoughts may hook you and distract you from being fully present in this exercise. This is *normal.* When you become aware that you've been sidetracked, gently bring your focus back to the exercise.

The more a person practices this, the more control they'll have over their thoughts and emotions.

What would have happened if I practiced Leaves On a Stream while I was a conspiracy theorist?

Practicing this exercise could have unraveled the stories I had been telling myself. Stories that were created by connecting the dots between totally unrelated events.

I could have escaped the grip of conspiracy theories far quicker if I had practiced cognitive defusion. Practicing it for five to ten minutes every morning would have given me a lot of clarity.

I would have recognized these stories as thoughts inside my head. Stories and thoughts that had no bearing on reality. These stories and thoughts are a perfect example of **The Map Is Not the Territory** concept from Chapter 7.

Anytime I felt anxiety or panic in my chest, I could have imagined placing it on a leaf and watching it float away.

That's the beauty of this technique. After you practice it for a little while you can do it on the fly. Instead of needing to close your eyes, you can simply *imagine* placing the thought or feeling on a leaf and letting it float away.

My hope and promise to you:

If you've ever experienced your loved one getting caught up in obsessive thoughts, you know how frightening this can be.

Rest assured: there is hope. Even if you run into resistance from your loved one, keep on keepin' on. Just keep showering them with love, curiosity, and compassion.

Yes, you can push them a little bit. Push too hard, and they might bite back.

If they're showing too much resistance to this technique? Turn to Chapter 11 and discover what getting wrapped up in these obsessive thoughts does for them.

Remember, it's the question of *"What does doing X do for you or allow you to feel or experience?"*

"What does focusing on these thoughts about the New World Order do for you or allow you to feel or experience?"

When you discover what engaging in conspiratorial beliefs does for them, help them find alternative ways to satisfy those emotional needs. Chapter 11 has some great ways to do this.

Once again, congrats for trucking along! This is a pretty heavy ass topic to say the least. More so when you see your family, friends, and loved ones slipping into madness.

With the right approaches and attitude you'll be able to rescue them.

So, keep your hope up. The Leaves On A Stream exercise can help protect your loved one from harmful and obsessive thoughts.

To get a guided meditation of Leaves On a Stream that your loved one can listen to, click the link below:

www.escapingtherabbithole.com/act

If you've ever struggled motivating your loved one to adopt healthier habits then you'll love the next chapter. I'm revealing a simple way to motivate them to adopt healthier habits or even implement some of the techniques in this book.

Chapter 14
Motivate a Conspiracy Theorist to Change

If you're struggling to convince your loved one to try some healthier habits or break away from some bad habits then this will be the most important thing you read in a long time.

Here's why:

It's extremely hard to motivate people to do something. Even if it's good for them and they want to do it.

Count your lucky stars that we've got an almost fool proof technique to motivate your loved one in this chapter.

Hopefully you have a list of healthier behaviors for your loved one to engage with. If not, consider revisiting some earlier chapters.

Let's say you've helped them discover healthier habits to engage in, such as the Hidden Benefits Technique, the Leaves On a Stream meditation, or some other habit. But they're resistant to trying them out?

First and foremost, you want to get some commitment from them to try these healthier habits, hobbies, behaviors, or actions.

But how do you do this? It's easier than you think.

Motivate your loved one to change their habits with Instant Influence

A lot of sales, persuasion, and influence techniques fall flat. Dr. Michael Pantalon created the Instant Influence technique. It works really well for encouraging someone to change their behavior. [8]

How?

Most persuasion techniques cause you to focus on a person's resistance or objection to taking action.

Taking on resistance is like butting up against a brick wall. Wouldn't you agree it's much better to look for a door in the wall or a crack you can shimmy your way through?

---

[8] Instant Influence – How to Get Anyone to Do Anything - Fast!, Michael V. Pantalon PhD

172

The three basic premises of Instant Influence are:

1) No one has to do anything. Their choice is entirely up to them to make.

2) We already have enough motivation.

3) Focusing on a tiny bit of motivation is better than breaking down the wall of resistance we just mentioned.

After they have a list of healthier habits you can start using this strategy right away.

If you've helped your loved one generate healthier habits but they're on the fence about using them, bust out this technique.

Here's the step-by-step process:

Step 1. Tell them the choice is theirs to make. *"I just want you to know; it's your choice to do X. It's not for me to decide. The choice is completely up to you."*

Step 2. Ask them, *"Why might you want to do X?"*

Step 3. Ask them, *"How ready are you to start doing X on a scale of 1 to 10?"*

Step 4. Ask them, *"Why didn't you pick a lower number?"*

Step 5. Ask them, *"Imagine you've changed and you're now doing X; what are the positive benefits or outcomes?"*

Step 6. Ask them, *"Why are these outcomes important to you?"*

Step 7. Ask them, *"What is the next step, if anything?"*

Let's break down how instant influence works:

Step 1. Tell them the choice is theirs to make.

We all want to feel like we have a say in our lives. We value our own personal autonomy. Personal autonomy is being able to make our own choices. This includes the freedom to pursue these choices.

When you tell someone, *"This is your choice to make,"* we take pressure off them. It becomes easier to influence someone because they feel like they now have a choice.

Read these two statements below and think about which one feels better.

"You need to finish reading this book if you want to help your loved one" versus *"I can't make this choice for you. It's your choice to read this book and see if it can help your loved one."*

Step 2. Ask them, *"Why might you want to do X?"*

If you were to ask, *"Why haven't you been doing X?"* it is a good way for them to drift into negative feelings or, God forbid, tell a negative story about why they can't accomplish something.

Asking someone, *"Why haven't you been doing X?"* also reinforces an external locus of control. Focusing on why they might want to do something pops them into an internal locus of control.

You're also not telling them what they need to do. Try to force a solution on someone and watch it backfire. Instead, ask them why they might want to do something, and they'll explain why.

Step 3. Ask them, *"How ready are you to start doing X on a scale of 1 to 10?"*

This question has a lot of implied magic behind it. You're not asking them if they're willing to change.

Instead, you're asking them how ready they are to change.

Everyone wants to have good things happen in their life—this includes losing weight, improving their relationships, starting new habits, etc.

Don't focus on what number they give you. Any number is good. Whatever number they give you represents their current readiness to change.

Step 4. Ask them, *"Why didn't you pick a lower number?"*

Talk about a sneaky question! Most people expect to hear, *"Why didn't you pick a higher number?"*

"He's gonna get tricky with me, and try to motivate me more by asking me why I didn't pick a higher number." most people think.

Watch their shock as you Bruce Lee that smug look clear off their face with your brilliant wordplay.

They'll tell you why they didn't pick a lower number and in turn justify their desire to do the new healthier habit, hobby, or behavior.

Step 5. Ask them, *"Imagine you've changed and you're now doing X. What would the positive benefits or outcomes be from this?"*

Your Jedi powers are already growing stronger, young Padawan. (Yes, I'm a huge nerd).

Anytime you ask someone to imagine something, you get them to stretch their mind as to what's possible.

Step 6. Ask them, *"Why are these outcomes important to you?"*

You're cutting right to the heart of what's most important to them; their desires and values. If they say, *"I want to be around for my family,"* follow up and dig deeper.

"Why is it important for you to be around for your family?"

"Because I want to keep them safe!"

And boom! You've hit the nail on the head.

Ultimately, they want to keep their family safe.

And lastly...

Step 7. Ask them, *"What is the next step, if anything?"*

This last question reinforces their ability to make their own choices. You're not telling them what they should do. You're giving them free rein.

Notice how this question also implies that they are the ones in control of what happens. It shifts them from an external to an internal locus of control.

Why?

Because they have to take action.

From here, you might have to help them cook up a game plan. If they're struggling trying to think of the next step they need to take, try to make some simple suggestions.

NOTE: To make this fun and slightly addicting, have them gamify their results.

Gamification is the process of taking addictive elements of games and applying them to nongame-related endeavors.

Humans have loved games for thousands of years. The earliest known board game was invented over 4,000 years ago!

So why go against the grain? Use something that humans have been hardwired to do.

I recommend checking out the free habit gamification app Habitica.

Habitica is a great way to build new habits. It's an RPG (role-playing game for non-nerds). Seriously check it out, if only for yourself. If your loved one likes games they'll dig Habitica.

Habitica can help shift someone from an external to an internal locus of control. By taking deliberate actions that satisfy their values, they'll gain more and more control of their life.

But before you introduce them to Habitica, they'll need habits to look forward to. So bust out your favorite magic writing stick and some paper.

Remember the values you helped them to discover in Chapter 11?

You do? Good, let's push on.

Help them to generate a big list of habits, behaviors, and actions that will get them to experience more of their values. Keep in mind the larger the list the better. More habits just mean more choices.

But don't go get all gung-ho and convince them to try everything all at once. You'll overwhelm them. Soon they'll be poppin' a doom balloon.

Take baby steps with them.

Help them identify two or three things they can do daily or weekly to experience more of their values.

If they're struggling to generate a list of things to do, turn to Chapter 11.

WOOP, There It Is

Remember the WOOP technique covered in Chapter 6? If your loved one has some habits they'd love to try but need help getting started, introduce them to WOOP.

Remember, WOOP stands for Wish, Outcome, Obstacle, and Plan.

Wish. This is the goal/habit they have.

Write their wish below or on separate paper in three to six words.

_____

_____

Outcome. What's the best possible result of them achieving this goal? In other words, how would achieving this goal make them feel?

_____

_____

What would be the best thing about fulfilling this wish? How would fulfilling this wish make them feel?

In three to six words below, write down the best possible outcome of achieving this wish:

_____

_____

Have them take a few minutes to visualize fulfilling this wish. Have them close their eyes and imagine achieving this goal. Have them feel those good feelings in their body as they imagine fulfilling their wish.

Obstacle. This is the inner obstacle that is likely to trip them up later. Have them identify what it is in them that would prevent them from achieving this wish.

What internal struggle or obstacle would stand in their way of fulfilling this wish? Write down the inner obstacle or struggle below or on another piece of paper in three to six words.

_____

_____

Have them close their eyes and imagine this inner obstacle getting in their way for a few minutes. Have them imagine this inner obstacle as fully as possible.

Plan. Time to create a conditional plan. Have them think of one action they can take to overcome this obstacle out in the wild.

Next, create an If/then plan with this action.

If [inner obstacle], then I will [action]

Example: If [_fear of failure_], then I will take [_three deep breaths_]

The formula is If [obstacle], then I will [action]

Have them write their if/then plan below or on a separate piece of paper:

If _____, then I will _____

Next, have them close their eyes. Have them imagine being in a future situation where they will likely experience that internal struggle.

They need to repeat this if/then plan mentally while they imagine engaging in this new action/behavior. Have them mentally repeat this over and over. Repeat the mantra of *"If [obstacle] then I will [action]"* while they imagine engaging in that action.

I'd suggest having them repeat this if/then plan at least 15 to 20 times.

Note: I'd highly suggest you encourage them to download the WOOP app on their phone. The app makes it a whole hell of a lot easier.

Want to have me guide you through the WOOP process and make it easier to understand? Watch the free video at the link below:

www.escapingtherabbithole.com/woop

A message of hope

You may feel like you just got force-fed from a fire hose. Yes, it's a lot of information to digest. Keep in mind that's all it is— information. Unless you take action and implement this stuff it's useless.

Give yourself props for making it this far in this book. You've made some significant progress!

If you want a better chance of rescuing your loved one from conspiracy theories, make sure to run yourself through all of the exercises in this book. If you've skipped over any of the interactive video exercises in this book, go back and do them.

I would also like to suggest that you use the various techniques/meditations in this book:

- The WOOP technique to set goals—chapters 6, 9 and 14
- The Instant Rapport technique in—chapter 8
- Leaves On a Stream meditation to stop racing thoughts—chapter 13
- Hidden Benefits Meditation—chapter 11
- Urge Surfing to bust up internet addictions—chapter 12

Go back through the book if you need too and most importantly—play like a kid and HAVE FUN!

Are we almost done on our journey? Hardly! The next chapter is an invitation to keep walking down this exciting path with yours truly.

Chapter 15
The Next Steps in Our Journey

Thanks for reading this book and coming along on is journey with me. What originally started as a passing thought months ago snowballed into this book you've been reading.

Many of my friends have encouraged me to write about my experiences as a conspiracy theorist.

Which brings my attention to you; if you've experienced having a loved one in conspiracy theories or a cult, you have a powerful story to share with others. Many families are being torn apart because of conspiracy theories and cults.

Your story might help other people who are struggling to heal. I would like to suggest that you write a book about your story.

Writing this book has been a therapeutic and healing process. It's helped me better understand how other people and I got sucked into conspiracy theories in the first place.

My friend and colleague, Dr. Richard Nongard, has told me a few times to write about my past as a conspiracy theorist.

In fact, his online workshop is responsible for this book being published.

If you have a book you've wanted to write, check out his website:

www.twelveweekbook.com

Our journey doesn't have to end here. To discover how I can help you transform your life, jump on over to the link below to schedule your 20-minute no-cost strategy call. We'll talk about how I can help you change your life with the power of hypnosis/life coaching.

www.escapingtherabbithole.com/call

I look forward to connecting with you.

Once again, thanks for reading this book.

Aloha,
Antonio

P.S. You're not paranoid if they're really out to get you ;)

P.P.S. Keep an eye out for more books from me. The next one will be a self-care guide for loved ones of conspiracy theorists and cult members. To know when it's published jump on the early bird list by going to the link below.

www.escapingtherabbithole.com/new

About The Author

Antonio Perez is a former conspiracy theorist turned certified hypnotist and life coach. He helps friends and family members of conspiracy theorists overcome stress, anxiety, and any other issues they're experiencing as a result of their loved one.

If you're experiencing any stress, anxiety, or any other issues because your loved one is trapped in conspiracy theories, schedule your no-cost 20-minute strategy call to discover how he can help you:

www.escapingtherabbithole.com/call

www.ingramcontent.com/pod-product-compliance
Lightning Source LLC
Chambersburg PA
CBHW060515130626
46553CB00002B/508